So you really want to learn

Junior Science
Book 2

GALORE PARK

So you really want to learn

Junior Science

Book 2

Sue Hunter and Jenny Macdonald

Editor: David Penter
Series Editor: Louise Martine

www.galorepark.co.uk

Published by Galore Park Publishing Ltd
19/21 Sayers Lane, Tenterden, Kent TN30 6BW
www.galorepark.co.uk

Layout by Typetechnique
Technical illustrations by Ian Moores
Cartoon illustrations by Rowan Barnes-Murphy

Printed by Replika Press, India

ISBN: 978 1905735 19 8

First published 2009, reprinted 2010

To accompany this course:
Junior Science Teacher's Resource
(available for download from www.galorepark.co.uk)

Details of other Galore Park publications are available at
www.galorepark.co.uk

ISEB Revision Guides, publications and examination papers may also be
obtained from Galore Park.

The following photographs are used by permission of the photo libraries as indicated.
All other images are copyright © Sue Hunter.

Page 1 Jiri Loun/Science Photo Library; page 2 Simon Fraser/Science Photo Library; page 12
Terry Smith Images Arkansas Picture Library/Alamy; page 16 (R) David Aubrey/Science
Photo Library; page 19 Daniel Sambraus/Science Photo Library; page 20 D. Roberts/Science
Photo Library; page 21 Claude Nuridsany & Marie Perennou/Science Photo Library; page 22
Science Photo Library; page 24 Andrew Syred/Science Photo Library; page 30 George
Ranalli/Science Photo Library; page 31 B.W. Hoffmann/Agstockusa/Science Photo Library;
page 36 (L) John Devries/Science Photo Library; page 36 (R) Dr Jeremy Burgess/Science
Photo Library; page 37 James H. Robinson/Science Photo Library; page 40 Claude Nuridsany
& Marie Perennou/Science Photo Library; page 41 (L) Keith M Law/Alamy, (R) Charles E
Mohr/Science Photo Library; page 56 J.G. Paren/Science Photo Library; page 57 Mark Sykes/
Science Photo Library; page 68 Andrew Lambert Photography/Science Photo Library; page
82 Duncan Shaw/Science Photo Library; page 83 Dr Dominic Hodgson, British Antarctic
Survey; page 88 Francoise De Mulder/Roger Viollet/Getty Images; page 96 Edward Kinsman/
Science Photo Library; page 98 Sheila Terry/Science Photo Library; page 100 (L &R) Emily
Hunter; pages 112 and 114 Jenny Macdonald; p122 (T) David Cannon/Getty Images (B)
Christopher Swann/Science Photo Library; page 124 Skyscan/Science Photo Library; page
129 NASA/Science Photo Library; page 131 NASA/JPL-CALTECH/Cornell University/
Science Photo Library; page 132 NASA/JPL/SSI/Science Photo Library; page 137 John
Sanford/Science Photo Library

About the authors

Sue Hunter has been a science teacher in a variety of schools for more years than she cares to remember. Her experiences have included teaching in a choir school and a London middle school, teaching GSCE and A level in the Netherlands and a short spell as a full-time mother of two. She is Head of Science at St Hugh's School in Oxfordshire and a member of the Common Entrance 11+ setting team. She has run a number of training courses for prep school teachers, including at Malvern College and for the Independent Association of Prep Schools (IAPS), and is currently IAPS Support Co-ordinator for science and a member of the Independent Schools Inspectorate.

Jenny Macdonald has been a teacher since graduating in 1973, teaching in both state and private schools, and for the last ten years has taught science to Years 3 to 6 at St Hugh's School in Oxfordshire. After marrying in the mid-1970s, she moved to Oxfordshire and in the 1980s the family acquired a smallholding where she raised three children before graduating to sheep, chickens, cats and dogs. She is a keen singer in several local choirs, enjoys outdoor pursuits and has travelled extensively, helping her husband undertake research work on wildlife conservation projects around the world.

Working safely

Suggestions for practical work in the 'To Do' sections may involve potential hazards and these have been highlighted with the symbol ⚠. Guidance on how to conduct practical work safely within the classroom environment is given in the Teacher's Resource which accompanies this book.

Note to teachers

The Teacher's Resource (available as a download or on CD) which accompanies this title contains valuable worksheets for the 'To do' exercises including a useful note on resources, lists of key vocabulary and topic summaries with learning objectives.

Preface

The most exciting phrase to hear in science, the one that heralds new discoveries, is not 'Eureka!' but 'That's funny ...' **Isaac Asimov**

The study of science for young children is a voyage of discovery. It stimulates their curiosity and provides a vehicle for them to explore their world, to ask questions about things that they observe and to make sense of their observations. It does not exist in isolation but draws upon many other aspects of a well-rounded curriculum and should be practical, interesting and, above all, fun.

This book is the second of three Junior Science books designed to be used in Years 3 to 5. The three books together can be used to underpin a course of study leading to the 11+ Common Entrance examinations and link directly into *So You Really Want to Learn Science* Books 1 and 2, by Ron Pickering. The books are designed in such a way that they can be used as a course in their own right, one book for each of Years 3 to 5, or as a resource to support an existing scheme of work.

Acknowledgements

We are immensely grateful to Louise Martine, Terry Hardy and Annette Bruno for their support in preparing this book and to David Penter for casting his expert eye over the script.

Thanks must also go to our families for putting up with erratically-timed meals, producing cups of coffee and tea or glasses of wine at appropriate moments and providing support and encouragement throughout the gestation period of the book.

Lastly, we should thank the pupils at St Hugh's School, Carswell, for (unwittingly) acting as guinea pigs for much of the material in the book. Their unfailing enthusiasm for science has been our inspiration and this book is for them.

Sue Hunter and Jenny Macdonald
September 2009

Contents

Chapter 5: Keeping warm, keeping cool

Chapter 6: Electrical circuits

Chapter 7: Friction

Chapter 8: Sun, Earth and Moon

Chapter 1: Habitats

What is a habitat?

A **habitat** is a place where an animal or plant lives. The group of plants and animals that live there is called a **community**. In order for a community to live and grow well, the habitat must provide three important things:

- It must provide a place to **feed**.

- It must provide a place of **shelter**.

- It must be a place where the animal or plant can **reproduce**.

Anywhere can be a habitat; it might be under a log in your garden, it might be a park, a pond, a woodland, a cemetery, the land beside a motorway or railway, or even a rubbish dump! Provided the animal can find food, shelter and be able to reproduce there, then it is a habitat.

Small habitats are often part of larger habitats. The habitat under a rock might be beside a pond, and the pond might be in a woodland.

How do habitats differ?

A tropical rainforest

Some habitats, such as tropical forests, provide homes and feeding places for many different kinds of plants and animals. Other habitats, for example, the Arctic, provide homes and feeding places for fewer kinds of plants and animals.

Some plants and animals can live very successfully in many different habitats. Plants and animals grow well in habitats where they are well **adapted**. For example, rabbits often live in large numbers on farmland, and yet they seem equally at home living in cemeteries, on open hillsides or even by the roadside. These are good habitats for rabbits because rabbits are adapted to eating grass and digging burrows to shelter and raise their young. Foxes might also live in all these different places because they are adapted to catching rabbits to eat.

Sometimes animals are found in very different habitats but behave differently in each one. For example, we often find gulls at the coast, flying over the sea and catching fish. However, we also find gulls inland a long way from the coast, feeding on rubbish that they find in rubbish tips, or following behind tractors and catching worms turned up by the plough. They have found ways of living successfully in different habitats, and we say they have changed their behaviour to find food in these different habitats.

Gulls pursuing a tractor in a half ploughed field

For a plant to grow successfully in its habitat it needs space to grow. It must be able to take the moisture and **minerals** it needs from the ground. It also needs to be able to take enough light **energy** from sunlight to make its own food. Some plants can only grow in particular places. For example, gorse bushes need very sandy soils but flag irises grow well in marshy areas beside ponds; ferns grow well in shade but sunflowers do better in bright sunny conditions. Other plants can grow in many kinds of habitats. For example, nettles will grow in good soil or in rubble or waste ground as long as they have enough light. Grasses grow almost everywhere and can survive well even when they are grazed by animals.

Exercise 1.1

Use the words in the box to fill in the gaps in the sentences below. Each word may be used once, more than once or not at all.

adapted	feed	anywhere	shelter	reproduce	community

1. In order for a habitat to be successful the plant or animal must be able to _____ , _____ and _____ .

2. The plants and animals in a habitat are called a _____ .

3. Almost _____ can be a habitat.

4. Animals and plants live and grow well in habitats that they are well _____ to.

Exercise 1.2

1. Explain what is meant by the word 'habitat'.

2. What do animals need in a habitat if they are to survive?

3. What do plants need in a habitat if they are to survive?

4. What is the name given to the group of plants and animals living in a habitat?

5. (a) Name three habitats where you might find gulls.

   (b) What sort of food might gulls be feeding on in each of these habitats?

6. What word is used to describe the way in which some plants and animals are able to change in order to survive in their habitats?

Looking closely at habitats

If you are quiet and look and listen carefully when you visit a habitat, you will discover that there are many different animals and plants for you to study. On the following pages there are pictures of two habitats you may have seen. You can read about just a few of the living organisms that can be found in them.

The first habitat is a churchyard (pages 6 and 7), which can be found in the town, city or countryside. A churchyard is usually a peaceful place, and provides animals and birds with a quiet area in which to feed, find shelter and to reproduce.

The second habitat is a rock pool (pages 8 and 9). You may have visited the seaside and spent some time looking in rock pools on the beach. A rock pool is a very exciting habitat. Here you will find some plants and animals that cannot survive out of water – they are safe in the pool when the tide has gone out. When the tide comes in again some of the animals will escape, others will arrive, and some will stay. So the community will be constantly changing.

Did you know?
Hermit crabs (see the rock pool picture on pages 8 and 9) are often found with sea anemones on their shells. The anemone helps to camouflage and protect the crab and will eat leftover scraps of the crab's food. When the crab moves to a new shell, it may move the anemone from one shell to the other.

Exercise 1.3

Look at the picture of a churchyard on pages 6 and 7 and use the information to help you to answer these questions.

1. Give the proper name for the homes of the following animals: badger, red fox, squirrel, rabbit.

2. Explain in your own words the meaning of the word 'hibernation'.

3. Name the animals in the churchyard picture that hibernate.

4. Name all the animals in the picture that have earthworms in their diet.

5. Make a list of all the animals in the picture that have some part of a plant in their diet.

6. Make a list of all the animals in the picture that catch and eat smaller animals such as mice and rabbits, insects and worms.

7. What is the meaning of the word 'nocturnal'?

8. Which of the animals in the picture are nocturnal?

9. Name an important difference between the yew tree and the oak tree.

10. (a) What is a mammal?

    (b) Make a list of all the mammals you can see in the picture.

. . . .

Exercise 1.4: Extension questions

1. Find out how owl feathers are different from other bird's feathers, so that they are able to fly silently at night.

2. (a) Bats are able to fly around in the dark without bumping into anything. Find out how they are able to do this.

    (b) What is the name given to this process?

    (c) Suggest why submarines use a similar method for navigating deep in the ocean.

. . . .

Exercise 1.5

Look at the picture of the rock pool on pages 8 and 9 and use the information to help you to answer these questions.

1. The barnacle and the limpet are animals that live in shells. Describe the ways in which they are similar, and the ways in which they are different.

2. The mussel also attaches itself to the rocks – how does it do this?

3. What is the food of the dog whelk?

4. Describe in your own words how the dog whelk feeds.

5. How are plant plankton and seaweed similar?

6. Why are plant plankton and seaweeds not found deep in the ocean?

7. Describe an important difference between a hermit crab and a shore crab.

8. Is the sea anemone a plant or an animal? Explain your answer.

Yew tree
(Evergreen tree)
Makes its own food using energy from the Sun.
Fruits contain seeds that are poisonous to people.
Birds and animals can eat the fruit safely.

Squirrel
(Mammal)
Feeds on seeds, nuts and buds and
stores food for the winter.
Makes a nest called a drey in trees.
Sleeps a lot in winter but does not
hibernate properly.

Rabbits
(Mammal)
Feed on grasses and other plants.
Have good eyesight and hearing.
Live underground in holes called
warrens.

Blackberry bush
Makes its own food using energy from the Sun.
Prickly bush with sweet juicy fruits.
Leaves and berries are eaten by many birds,
mammals and invertebrates.
Safe place for nesting birds.

Fungi
Are not plants because they cannot make their own food.
Decompse dead plants and animals and return minerals
to the soil.
Provide food for small animals.

Churchyard habitat

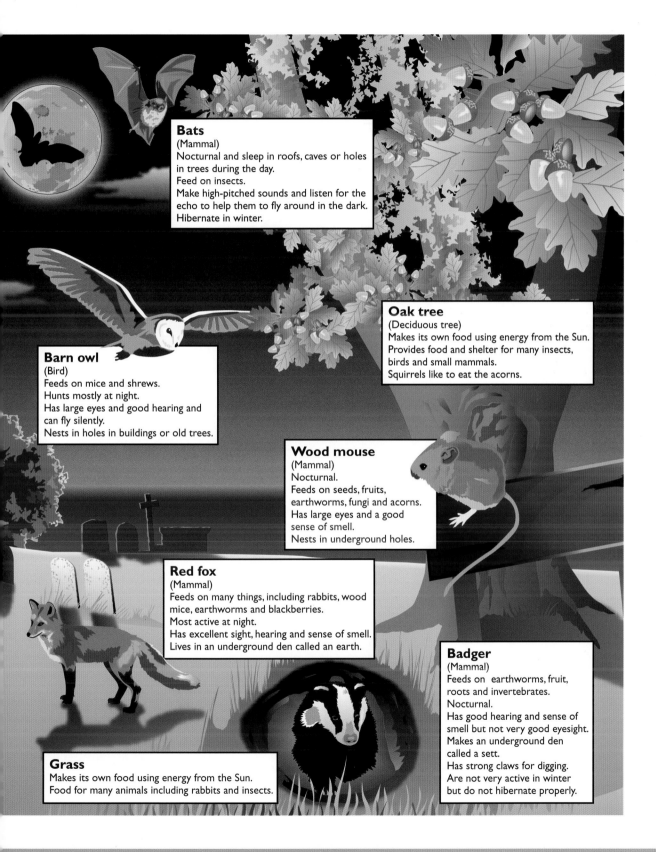

Bats
(Mammal)
Nocturnal and sleep in roofs, caves or holes in trees during the day.
Feed on insects.
Make high-pitched sounds and listen for the echo to help them to fly around in the dark.
Hibernate in winter.

Oak tree
(Deciduous tree)
Makes its own food using energy from the Sun.
Provides food and shelter for many insects, birds and small mammals.
Squirrels like to eat the acorns.

Barn owl
(Bird)
Feeds on mice and shrews.
Hunts mostly at night.
Has large eyes and good hearing and can fly silently.
Nests in holes in buildings or old trees.

Wood mouse
(Mammal)
Nocturnal.
Feeds on seeds, fruits, earthworms, fungi and acorns.
Has large eyes and a good sense of smell.
Nests in underground holes.

Red fox
(Mammal)
Feeds on many things, including rabbits, wood mice, earthworms and blackberries.
Most active at night.
Has excellent sight, hearing and sense of smell.
Lives in an underground den called an earth.

Badger
(Mammal)
Feeds on earthworms, fruit, roots and invertebrates.
Nocturnal.
Has good hearing and sense of smell but not very good eyesight.
Makes an underground den called a sett.
Has strong claws for digging.
Are not very active in winter but do not hibernate properly.

Grass
Makes its own food using energy from the Sun.
Food for many animals including rabbits and insects.

Barnacle
Fixes itself firmly to rocks and does not move.
Feeds by fanning its bristly legs through the top of the shell to catch plankton.
When the tide goes out it seals its shell trapping air and water inside.

Mussel
Has two shells that can close tightly using a strong muscle.
Fixes itself to rocks with strong threads.
Feeds by sucking in water and eating the plankton.
Usually found in large groups which helps to protect them from the waves.

Prawn
Feeds on plankton.
Hides in cracks in the rocks.
Is most active at night.
Can swim backwards.
Can change the brightness of its body colour to camouflage itself.

Plankton
Very tiny (microscopic) plants and animals that float around in the water.
Plant plankton make their own food using energy fom the Sun.
Provide food for many animals.

Dog whelk
Feeds on mussels, limpets and barnacles.
Feeds by drilling a hole through the shells of its prey and then sucking out the soft parts of the animal inside.
Those that feed on mussels become dark coloured and those that feed on barnacles become white.

Shore crab
Feeds on dead animals.
Have five pairs of legs.
The front pair of legs have sharp stong claws for holding food and cracking open shells.
Have eyes on short stalks which can be pulled into the shell for safety.

Rock pool habitat

Herring gull
Eats almost anything, including dead animals
and the remains of other animals' food.
Eats shelly animals by dropping them from
a height onto rocks to break the shell.
Nests on ledges on the cliffs.

Limpet
Clings to rocks with a large sucker-like foot for protection
from predators and to avoid being swept away by waves.
Moves slowly over the rocks eating microscopic plants.

Sea anemone
Fixes itself to the rocks or the
shells of hermit crabs.
Feeds on small fish, prawns
and other small animals.
Feeds by catching its prey
using stinging tentacles and
then drawing it into its mouth.
Withdraws its tentacles and
looks like a blob of jelly when
the tide goes out.

Seaweed
Makes its own food using energy from the Sun.
Can only grow in shallow water where there is
enough sunlight.
Provides food and shelter for other plants and
animals in the rock pool.

Hermit crab
Feeds on dead plants and animals.
Does not have a shell of its own but uses the
shells of other animals.
Changes its shell from time to time as it grows.

Exercise 1.6: Extension question

Describe in your own words the relationship between the hermit crab and the sea anemone and explain how they benefit each other.

To do: Investigate a habitat

Look around the area where you live and try to identify some different habitats. Maybe you have woodland, fields or moorland near you. If you live in a town, there will be lots of habitats in your local park or even in your garden. Here are some suggestions of habitats for you to study. An identification book or key for the kinds of animals and plants you will find in the habitat will be useful.

Remember that a habitat is the home for a community of plants and animals. Take care of it when you are studying it and try to leave everything exactly as you found it. Remember to wash your hands straight away after doing fieldwork.

Under a log

Try to find an old log rotting on the ground, and carefully lift it up. Very gently lift away pieces of bark and look underneath. Hunt through the soil and any dead leaves that you find around the log.

Try to identify any creatures that you see. Use a soft paintbrush or a spoon to move the creatures gently, and use a hand lens to help you to see the animals more closely.

When you have finished with the log, remember that it must be carefully replaced exactly where you found it. It is a habitat, and the animals must be allowed to return to it.

Shake a tree

Find a leafy bush or tree and spread an old sheet on the ground underneath it. Carefully shake one or two of the branches above the sheet. You need to shake firmly but be careful not to damage the bush or tree. You will find that many of the small animals that live in the bush or tree will fall off onto the sheet.

Use a soft paintbrush or spoon to move the animals to a small container so that you can look at them closely with a hand lens. Try to identify the animals.

When you have finished, tip the animals gently off the sheet under the tree. They will quickly find their way back into the branches.

Pond dipping

Pond dipping is always fun, but remember that water can be dangerous so make sure an adult is nearby if you are dipping in a real pond. An open water butt or rainwater barrel makes a good little pond if you do not have a real pond near you.

Get a shallow container ready by putting some water from the pond into it. A white one is best or maybe a clear one with a sheet of white paper underneath it. Use a small net and move it slowly through the water.

Gently turn out the animals you find into the shallow container of water so that you can look at what you have caught. Try to identify the animals.

When you have finished, carefully lower the container into the pond so that the animals can be returned gently. Do not pour them back from a height as that could damage or even kill them.

Signs of larger animals

The animals you find in the first three activities will mostly be invertebrates. It is harder to study the vertebrate animals in your habitat because they hide or move away when we come near them. You may, however, be able to spot birds. Which birds can you find in your habitat? Can you think of a way to identify birds that you cannot see? Maybe you can tempt them to come a little closer if you put out some food for them. You will need to hide indoors or sit very still when watching them.

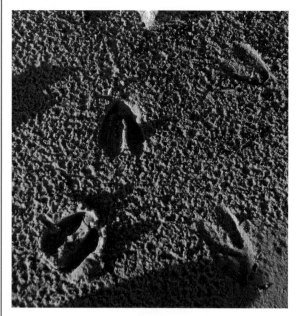
Deer tracks. Tracks are often the only way we can tell if an animal is present in a habitat

Larger wild animals, such as mammals, are much harder to spot. You may see a squirrel in the trees because they are quite bold, but you are less likely to see a deer, a field mouse or a grass snake. Instead, you need to look for signs that they have been there. Look for tracks in soft ground, nibbled nuts or acorns or maybe bark chewed off the trees. There are many more animals in your habitat than you realise.

Don't forget that the plants in the habitat are also part of the community. How many different species can you find and identify?

To do: How old is the tree?

You can work out the age of a felled tree by counting the annual rings that you see on a sawn cross-section of the trunk. The bark is the outer protective layer of the trunk, and underneath there is a thin layer of living cells called the cambium. Every year these cells divide and make a new layer of wood so the trunk grows outwards, making another annual ring. The tree becomes a little bit thicker and stronger every year. If the weather is dry the annual ring will be narrow. If the weather is wet the ring will usually be wider. You can count the number of rings to estimate the age of the tree.

You can also estimate the age of a tree that is living and growing without sawing it down. Every year, as the cambium makes a new layer of wood, the tree grows a little thicker – about 2.5 centimetres fatter each year.

1. Measure around the girth of the tree with a tape measure, at about 1 metre above the ground level, and note down the number of centimetres.

2. Using a calculator, divide the girth of your tree by 2.5 and the answer will be the approximate number of years that your tree has been growing.

Food chains

The plants and animals that make up the community in a habitat all depend on each other to survive. Sometimes two living organisms can live together, both benefiting each other. An example of this is the hermit crab and the sea anemone we saw in the rock pool habitat. In most cases, however, one organism will be eaten by another. We can show the feeding relationships between living organisms in diagrams called **food chains**.

All living organisms need energy in order to live and grow. Plants need the light energy from the Sun, which they use to make their own food using water from the soil and carbon dioxide from the air. They also take mineral salts from the soil to help them to keep healthy. Every time an animal does anything, such as run, jump, breathe or keep warm, it uses energy. Animals get their energy from the food they eat. A food chain shows how food, and therefore energy, is passed from one organism to another. Food chains begin with plants and end with animals.

Producers

Plants are called **producers** because they produce or make their own food. They use the energy from sunlight to join carbon dioxide and water to make sugar and release oxygen in a process called **photosynthesis**. (See Chapter 2)

Consumers

Animals are **consumers**. They cannot make their own food, so they consume (eat) other plants and animals. This food gives them the energy they need for life.

There are three kinds of consumers:

- **Herbivores** – animals that eat only plants.

- **Carnivores** – animals that eat only animals.

- **Omnivores** – animals that eat plants and animals.

Building a food chain

The first living organism in a food chain is a plant. This is because plants are the only organisms that can trap the light energy from sunlight and turn it into food energy.

The next link in the chain will be a consumer, a herbivore, which eats the leaves, roots, flowers or fruits of the plant to give it the energy it needs to live. The energy in the plant which the consumer eats will be passed on to the animal.

Next in the chain will be another consumer. This will be a carnivore: an animal that eats meat. The carnivore will catch and eat the herbivore, and the energy from what it eats will give it the energy it needs to find more food, to escape from danger and to grow and reproduce. Sometimes the first carnivore will be eaten by a second carnivore. There may be even more carnivores in the chain, although this doesn't happen often. The last carnivore in the chain is called the top carnivore, and is usually a large animal.

Remember that an omnivore eats both plant and animal material, so could be found at any level of a food chain acting as a herbivore or carnivore.

We draw a food chain by linking the living organisms together by arrows. When we draw the arrows in a food chain, it is important that they show the direction in which the food energy is travelling. The arrow means 'is eaten by'.

| grass | is eaten by → | rabbit | is eaten by → | fox |

There can be many food chains in a habitat, and they can often change, depending on the organisms that are available to be eaten. For example, a woodland habitat might include these food chains.

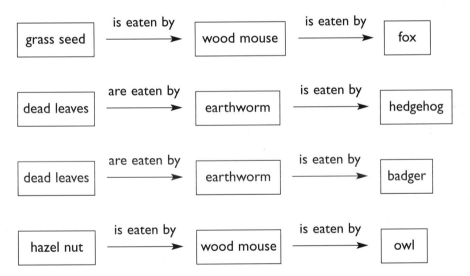

| grass seed | is eaten by → | wood mouse | is eaten by → | fox |

| dead leaves | are eaten by → | earthworm | is eaten by → | hedgehog |

| dead leaves | are eaten by → | earthworm | is eaten by → | badger |

| hazel nut | is eaten by → | wood mouse | is eaten by → | owl |

Can you identify the herbivores and carnivores in these food chains?

Even though the leaves are dead, they came from producers and so can start a food chain.

Can you identify the food chain in this picture?

Food chains can also vary in length.

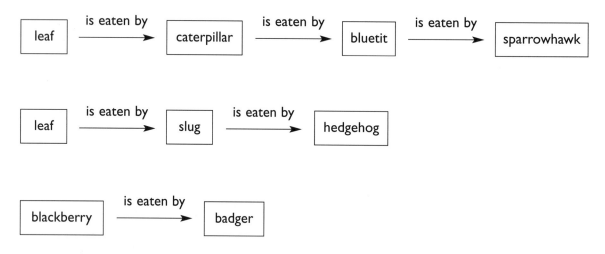

| leaf | is eaten by → | caterpillar | is eaten by → | bluetit | is eaten by → | sparrowhawk |

| leaf | is eaten by → | slug | is eaten by → | hedgehog |

| blackberry | is eaten by → | badger |

Can you think of a reason why some food chains are longer than others?

Predators and prey

Cheetahs are predators

When an animal catches other animals to eat, we call it a **predator**. The animal that is eaten is called the **prey**. Predators may have sharp claws, teeth or beaks to grasp their prey. Their eyes are usually on the front of their heads, facing forwards. This allows them to judge distances very well.

Prey animals often have their eyes on the sides of their heads. This gives them a better view all round so they can watch out for predators as they feed and move around.

A rabbit's eyes are on the side of its head so it can watch for predators

Did you know?
Some predators can run very fast but this uses a lot of energy. A cheetah can run at speeds of up to 30 metres per second (nearly 110 km per hour or 70 miles per hour). However, it can run like this only for a very short time. Most of the chases for prey are unsuccessful because the prey animals, such as gazelle, are also fast runners and dodge around making it hard for the cheetah to catch them.

Some animals feed on the bodies of animals that have already died. We call these animals **scavengers**. Examples of scavengers are magpies and crows, which are often seen eating the bodies of animals that have been killed on the roads. However, large carnivores, such as lions, will also scavenge dead animals if they can because it is easier than catching the prey for themselves. Scavengers play a useful role in clearing away the bodies of dead animals quickly. Without them we would have to wait for the decomposers to break down the bodies slowly.

Bacteria and fungi are **decomposers**. They feed on the remains of dead plants and animals, breaking them down into smaller parts – decomposing them. This helps to return minerals to the soil where they can be taken up by plants.

Vultures are scavengers

Exercise 1.7

Use the words in the box to complete the following sentences. Each word may be used once, more than once or not at all.

plants	carnivores	photosynthesis	omnivores	food
energy	producers	consumers	meat	herbivore

1. In a food chain, plants are described as _____ because they can make their own _____ using the process called _____ .

2. Animals need food to provide them with _____ .

3. In a food chain, animals are described as _____ .

4. A _____ is an animal that eats plant material.

5. Animals that only eat other animals are called _____ .

6. Omnivores eat _____ and _____ .

Exercise 1.8

1. Explain why food chains start with a plant.

2. What do plants need to make their food?

3. What is the difference between a herbivore and an omnivore?

4. What do the arrows in a drawing of a food chain mean?

5. What is a predator?

6. Why do predators generally have their eyes on the front of their heads?

7. Rabbits have their eyes on the sides of their heads. What does this suggest about their position in a food chain?

8. What word is used to describe animals that eat the remains of dead animals?

9. Look at the picture of a churchyard on pages 6 and 7. Use the information to draw two different food chains for this habitat.

Exercise 1.9: Extension questions

1. Look at the picture of the rock pool habitat on pages 8 and 9. Find as many food chains as you can and draw them out neatly.

2. Look carefully at your drawings of food chains. Which animals would be affected if there was no plankton in the water? Remember to think about the whole food chain.

To do: Design a predator

Choose a habitat to discuss. It might be one shown in this chapter or you could choose another, such as the Arctic or the deep sea.

Design a new predator to hunt in your habitat. Discuss with your partner or your class what characteristics would help it to hunt and catch food. Think about its colour, eyesight, size, the type of habitat that it is hunting in and anything else you can think of to make it a good predator. Draw a picture of your animal and label its important characteristics.

If you have time you could design a prey animal for your predator. What characteristics would help it to detect danger and to escape? Maybe you and your class could make a wall display using your pictures.

The right teeth for the job

In *Junior Science Book 1* you learnt about the different types of teeth in our mouths. (See Book 1, page 13.) Can you remember them all? Different animals eat different food, and so need different sorts of teeth.

Herbivores eat only plant material so they need strong **incisor** teeth at the front of their mouths that can cut tough leaves or branches. They also have big **grinding** teeth at the back of their mouths to help them to chew it all. They do not need sharp canines. If you look at the teeth of a herbivore such as a horse, you can see there is a gap where other animals might have canine teeth.

A horse's skull

Horses have large **molar** teeth at the back of the upper and lower jaws on each side. These have ridges that make them adapted to grinding tough plant material. The chewed plant material is easier for the animal to **digest**.

Predators, such as lions and foxes, have sharp **canine** teeth to help them catch and hold their prey and to tear the meat from the carcass. Animals that eat insects or fish often have lots of little sharp teeth to help them catch and eat their prey.

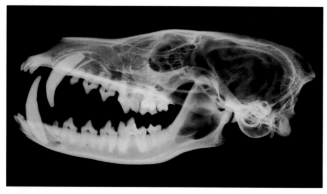

X-ray of the skull of a red fox

Foxes are carnivores. They have very sharp canine teeth which are good for holding and **ripping** the meat it has just caught. Further back in their mouths they have teeth that work like scissors, for cutting up tough meat. These are called **carnassial** teeth.

Did you know?
Animals that eat insects are called **insectivores**. An example of an insectivore is a shrew, which is a small animal that is very energetic so it needs a lot of food. A shrew has to eat 1½ times its own body weight in insects each day to get enough energy to survive. That's about the same as you eating 30–40 kg of food each day!

Omnivores, such as badgers and humans, eat both plant and animal material so they need **biting**, **tearing** and **chewing** teeth. Humans have sharp incisors for biting, strong canines for ripping and broad molars for grinding – all useful for the wide variety of different foods we eat.

If you look very carefully at a mammal's teeth you can probably work out what sort of food it eats. Once you know that, you can then work out lots of things about the way it lives.

To do: What do they eat?

Collect some pictures of animal skulls from books or the internet. You may even be lucky enough to have some real ones to look at.

Carefully look at the shape of the teeth in each skull. Try to work out the type of food that the animal eats. Is it a herbivore, a carnivore or an omnivore?

Plants can consume animals too!

There are some plants that live in areas where either the soil is very thin, or it is of poor quality and does not contain many minerals. These plants have developed a special trick. They catch insects and other small animals, and digest them. In this way they take in the minerals they are unable to get from the soil.

One kind of **carnivorous** plant is the pitcher plant. Some of its leaves have changed so they are rolled into a deep cup-shape, like a pitfall trap. The sides of the cup are very slippery and there is liquid in the bottom. Insects that land on the trap slip down into the cup and drown in the liquid. The liquid slowly digests the insects and the plant absorbs the minerals that are released.

Another carnivorous plant is the Venus flytrap, which has sensitive hairs on special leaves. When an insect walks over the leaf, it touches the hairs and triggers the leaves to snap shut, trapping the insect inside. The leaf then releases chemicals that digest the insect.

There are other plants with sticky leaves that trap insects, and plants that have a one-way route with forward pointing hairs that stop the insect from turning around and escaping.

Pitcher plant and beetles

Portrait of Charles Darwin, British naturalist

Charles Darwin was a famous British scientist who carried out many experiments using plants in his garden and greenhouse. He wanted to find out whether carnivorous plants could eat everything that lands on their traps. He tried feeding Venus flytraps all sorts of different foods. He gave them tiny pieces of foods like meat, egg or fruit, and drops of sugar solution. He found that the flytraps closed quickly around foods that were high in protein but did not close at all round the sugar solution. It seems that Venus flytraps can detect what is good for them!

. . . .

Exercise 1.10

Use the words in the box to fill in the gaps in the sentences below. Each word may be used once, more than once or not at all.

| molar   tear   canine   incisor   cut   grind   carnivorous |

1. Herbivores have sharp incisor teeth to _____ plant material and large _____ teeth to grind the leaves.

2. Carnivores need sharp _____ teeth to _____ meat.

3. Omnivores have _____ , _____ , and _____ teeth because they eat all kinds of food.

4. Pitcher plants and Venus flytraps are examples of _____ plants.

Exercise 1.11

1. Describe how you might tell the difference between a herbivore's skull and a carnivore's skull.

2. What name is given to animals that eat insects?

3. Why do small insect-eating animals need to eat relatively large amounts of food?

4. Why do some plants need to trap and digest insects?

5. Name two types of plants that can trap insects.

6. Describe in your own words how one of the plants you have mentioned in your answer to question 5 traps insects.

7. What experiment did Charles Darwin carry out using carnivorous plants? Describe in your own words what he did and what he discovered.

Chapter 2: Plants

All living organisms need **energy** for activity and growth. The energy they need comes from their **food**. As we saw in Chapter 1, all animals fit somewhere in a food chain by eating other animals, plants or a mixture of animals and plants. Can you remember what is the first link in the food chain?

Plants lead the way

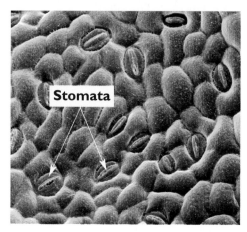

If you look at the underside of a leaf with a microscope you can see the holes called stomata; here you can see stomata on a rose leaf

Plants are always at the beginning of food chains because, unlike animals, they can make their own food. They make their food by joining **carbon dioxide**, taken from the air, with water from the soil, using light energy from the Sun. Light is trapped in the green pigment (colouring), called **chlorophyll**, in their leaves. The food that plants make from these ingredients is a sugar called **glucose**. This process is called **photosynthesis**. At the same time as making **glucose**, plants make **oxygen**. This escapes through little holes, called **stomata**, in their leaves.

Without the energy from sunlight, plants would not be able to make their food. Can you think what might happen to the animals on Earth if there was no sunlight?

Plants are not only important for being at the start of food chains, they are also important for providing the oxygen we need to breathe from the air. Almost all living things including plants need oxygen from the air to release the energy they need from their food. This process is called **respiration**. During daylight, green plants take carbon dioxide from the air to make their own food by photosynthesis, and in exchange they give out oxygen. Indeed plants have made all the Earth's oxygen by photosynthesis. People and other animals breathe in the oxygen that they need and breathe out the carbon dioxide that the plants need. Without this partnership between plants and animals there would be no life on Earth.

Green plants also take oxygen from the air for respiration and give out carbon dioxide. However, green plants make more oxygen during daylight by photosynthesis than they use in respiration, so there is still enough for us and for everything else that breathes oxygen.

. . . .

Exercise 2.1

Use the words in the box to fill in the gaps in the sentences below. Each word may be used once, more than once or not at all.

glucose	cannot	photosynthesis	energy	carbon dioxide
water	minerals	food	light	plants	oxygen

1. All living organisms need _____ for activity and growth.

2. The energy that living organisms need comes from their _____ .

3. _____ are always at the beginning of the food chain because they can make their own _____ .

4. Animals _____ make their own food.

5. Plants need _____ from the Sun, _____ from the air and _____ from the soil to make their own food.

6. The food that a plant makes is a sugar called _____ .

7. Animals breathe in _____ and breathe out _____ .

8. During photosynthesis plants take in _____ from the air and give out oxygen.

Exercise 2.2

1. Why does a food chain start with a plant?

2. What is the name given to the process that plants use to make their own food?

3. (a) What is the name of the green pigment in plant leaves?

   (b) What does this green pigment do?

4. What would happen to life on Earth if there were no sunlight?

5. (a) Which gas do most living organisms need to take from the air to help them obtain energy from food?

   (b) What name is given to the process by which living organisms release energy from food?

Exercise 2.3: Extension question

Design a poster to show how plants and animals depend on each other. Use the terms photosynthesis, respiration, oxygen, carbon dioxide and food chain in your poster.

What do we do?

Each part of the plant has a very important job to do. Together these parts enable the plant to carry out all the processes that will keep it alive and healthy.

What is the role of the flower?

- The **flower** is necessary for **reproduction** (making **seeds** that will grow into new plants).

- The flower may be bright and scented to attract insects, or dull if it does not need to attract insects.

What is the role of the leaves?

- The leaves are the places where the plant makes its food by photosynthesis. Leaves are often wide and flat to catch as much light as possible. They also contain the green pigment (**chlorophyll**) to trap energy from the Sun.

- The surface of the leaf has tiny holes (stomata) where carbon dioxide enters and oxygen exits the plant.

What is the role of the stem?

- The stem holds the flower in a good position for pollination.

- It holds the leaves in a good position to absorb light from the Sun.

- It carries water and minerals around the plant.

What is the role of the roots?

- The roots hold the plant firmly in the ground.

- They take in water and minerals from the soil.

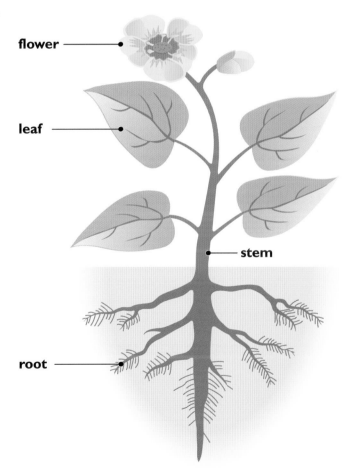

flower

leaf

stem

root

All the parts of the plant have different jobs to do

Exercise 2.4

Use the words in the box to fill in the gaps in the sentences below. Each word may be used once, more than once or not at all.

food	water	photosynthesis	hold	energy	minerals
transports	root	seeds	chlorophyll	reproduction	

1. The roots _____ the plant firmly in the ground, and take _____ and _____ from the soil.

2. The leaf is where the plant makes _____ . This process is called _____ .

3. The green pigment in leaves is called _____ . This absorbs _____ from sunlight.

4. The stem _____ water and _____ throughout the plant.

5. The role of the flower is to produce _____ that will grow in to new plants. This process is called _____ .

Exercise 2.5

1. Which part of a plant is responsible for taking in water?

2. How does water get from the part you have named in Question 1 to the rest of the plant?

3. Why do plants produce flowers?

4. Where does a plant make most of its food?

5. How does the plant take in carbon dioxide?

6. How does a plant make sure that its leaves are held in a good position to absorb energy from the Sun?

Exercise 2.6: Extension question

Each of the plant parts named above is important to the plant. However, there are some plants that do not produce flowers, some that have no leaves, some that have no stems and some that do not have roots.

See if you can find examples of plants that do not have each of the parts. Can you explain how each plant manages without them?

. . . .

Plants are everywhere

Scientists think there are about 350 000 different kinds of plants in the world, but only about 290 000 have so far been identified. These different kinds of plants are called **species**. They come in all shapes and sizes, with some trees growing to over 100 metres tall and other plants so small that you need a microscope to see them.

Plants grow almost everywhere, from mountains to swamps, and from deserts to the oceans. Those that are adapted to their habitat grow well and reproduce. However, habitats are changing and some habitats are disappearing. Many species of wild plant are not well adapted to the new habitats and are struggling to survive. These species are said to be endangered. If we do not look after them by preserving their habitats, some will disappear completely. They will become extinct.

A few thousand years ago, most of Europe, America and Asia was covered in forest. Many of these forest areas have now been destroyed but still nearly a third of the land on Earth is covered by forest. Forests will grow naturally wherever there is enough water. You do not find forests in the polar regions (near the North and South poles) because it is too cold and all the water is frozen as ice.

There are two main types of tree: deciduous and evergreen. **Deciduous** trees usually have broad flat leaves. Most deciduous trees lose all their leaves in autumn. The leaves often turn beautiful colours before they fall. After a winter rest, deciduous trees grow new leaves in spring when the weather is warmer and there is enough sunshine and rain. Examples of deciduous trees are oak and horse chestnut. Most deciduous trees grow in parts of the world where the summers are long and warm, and the winters are not very cold.

The leaves on these deciduous trees have changed colour and will soon fall

Evergreen trees keep their leaves for several years, and then lose them gradually while growing new ones to take their place. This means that they are never bare. The leaves on evergreen trees are usually tough and often waxy, and may be broad and flat or needle-shaped. Many trees in the rainforests are evergreen and many of them have huge broad leaves. The leaves on holly trees are also broad but they are very tough and waxy to help them cope with colder weather. Conifers, such as pine and spruce, have thin, waxy, needle-shaped leaves and are found in cold places with snowy winters. Can you explain why needle-shaped leaves would be an advantage in these conditions?

Exercise 2.7

Use the words in the box to fill in the gaps in the sentences on the next page. Each word may be used once, more than once or not at all.

needles	water	third	evergreen	growing	flat	cold
leaves	broad	deciduous	losing	snowy		

1. Nearly one _____ of the land is covered in forests.

2. Trees do not grow in the polar regions because the _____ is frozen.

3. There are two main types of tree called _____ and _____ .

4. Most deciduous trees lose all their _____ in the autumn.

5. Evergreen trees are always _____ new leaves to replace old ones.

6. The leaves of a deciduous tree are usually _____ and _____ .

7. Conifer trees have thin needle-shaped leaves and are found in _____ and _____ places.

· ·

First comes the seed

Many plants produce seeds that grow into new plants. Each seed contains an **embryo** (baby) plant and a store of food. The little plant needs this food to give it energy to start growing, and to keep it growing until it is able to start making food for itself.

We call the first stage of growth **germination**. The first thing to grow is the root. It pushes out of the seed and burrows down into the soil. Here the root can start to take in moisture from the soil. The root continues to grow and helps to fix the plant in the ground. At the same time it draws more moisture and minerals from the soil.

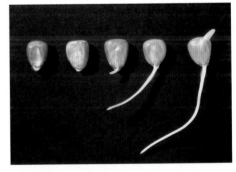

When a seed germinates, the root grows first; this photo shows a maize seedling

The next part to grow is the **shoot**, the part of the plant that will become the leaves and stem. This pushes out of the soil and turns upwards towards the sunlight. As the shoot grows it quickly sprouts leaves which open wide in order to trap sunlight in the green chlorophyll. As the plant grows, the stem gets taller and stronger to provide support for the leaves and later for the flowers and fruits.

The new plant can continue growing, even if it has used up its store of food from the seed, because it can produce its own food by photosynthesis.

To do: Germinating seeds

You will need:
- clean glass jar
- roll of blotting paper or kitchen paper
- 2 or 3 bean or pea seeds
- water

1. Soak your seeds in water for 24 hours.

2. Roll your paper and slide it into the jar.

3. Carefully wedge the seeds halfway down, resting them between the paper and the jar so you can see them clearly.

4. Pour some water into the bottom of the jar, just enough to moisten the paper, but not deep enough to touch the seed.

5. Now wait and observe your seeds over the next few days.
- Which part of the plant grows first?
- Which part grows next?
- You could measure the growth of the roots or shoots, and record your results on a bar chart, showing how much your plant has grown each day.

Don't forget to water your plant!

To do: Tricky business

If you plant another seed in another glass jar, you could try this experiment.

1. When you have put your seed in the jar and moistened the paper, tip out the rest of the water and put the lid loosely on the jar.

2. Now lay the jar on its side. You could make a little roll of modelling clay to stop it rolling around.

3. When the root has started to grow and is pointing downwards, lift your jar and turn it over so that the root is now pointing upwards.

4. Watch it over the next few days and see what happens.

Don't forget to keep the paper moist, or your plant will die.

Exercise 2.8

Use the words in the box to fill in the gaps in the sentences below. Each word may be used once, more than once or not at all.

root	new	shoot	moisture	leaves	germination	minerals

1. The role of the seed is to grow into a _____ plant.

2. This first stage of growth is called _____ .

3. The _____ grows first and takes in _____ and _____ from the soil.

4. The _____ grows next and quickly sprouts _____ .

. . . .

Exercise 2.9

1. Where does a seed get its energy from so that it can start growing?

2. What is meant by the term 'embryo'?

3. What are the two important jobs of the roots?

4. Why does the new plant need to grow leaves as quickly as possible?

. . . .

Exercise 2.10: Extension question

Does a seed need light in order to grow? Think carefully about your answer. You may be able to discuss what you think with a friend or your class. Then draw a labelled set of pictures to illustrate your answer.

To do: The WOW factor!

In this chapter you have learnt about some of the things that seeds and growing plants need in order to survive. In this experiment you will discover which of these things are needed by a seed when it is germinating.

1. Take a small container and put damp kitchen paper, blotting paper or potting compost in the bottom.

2. Add a little water to the container to make the paper or compost damp but not soggy.

3. Sprinkle some mustard or cress seeds into the container and then place it on a warm sunny windowsill.

4. If possible, count how many seeds you have added.

   You have probably grown seeds like this before and found they germinated very well. We call this the **control**. The purpose of the control is to provide something to compare your other tests with, to see if the seeds germinate as well as the control.

Think about what conditions you have given the seeds in your control experiment:

Control conditions	
Condition	
Water	✓
Paper or soil to support the plants	✓
Warm on windowsill	✓
Light coming through window	✓
Plenty of air so plants can take any gas they need easily	✓

How many of these conditions do you think are really necessary for the seed to germinate? Remember that germination is the stage when the seed breaks open and the root begins to form. A germinating seed has no leaves.

5. To test whether each condition is necessary, you need to set up a test exactly like your control but take away one of the conditions. For example, to find out if the seeds need water, set up the container in exactly the same way as the control but leave the paper or soil dry.

Think about how you can take away each of the other conditions to find out if they are necessary. If you counted your control seeds, use the same number in each test.

Test 1

Condition

Water	✗
Paper or soil to support the plants	✓
Warm on windowsill	✓
Light coming through window	✓
Plenty of air so plants can take any gas they need easily	✓

---

6. Leave your seeds for a few days, remembering to keep them moist, apart from the test where you have taken away the water.

7. Look at the seeds every day and compare all the tests with the seeds in the control experiment. If you counted your seeds, you can record the number that have germinated each day and your results can be shown on a graph or bar chart.

8. After two or three days, you should be able to decide whether taking each of the conditions away from the seeds has stopped them germinating successfully.

We have called this section of the chapter 'The WOW factor'. WOW is a good way of remembering what conditions the seeds needed to germinate. Can you explain why?
(See pages 24 and 25)

The seeds have germinated

If you like, you could keep the experiment going for a bit longer to see what happens when the little plants get their first leaves. Do you think the little seedlings will need the same conditions as the germinating seeds?

What comes next? – Flower power!

In Chapter 1 you learnt that living organisms must be able to feed, to find a safe place to live and to reproduce if they are to survive well in their habitats.

You have learnt already in this chapter that plants are able to make their own food as long as they have carbon dioxide, moisture and sunlight. We have also learnt that the seeds they produce will grow into new plants, but how do plants make their seeds?

Roses have brightly coloured petals

Many plants grow flowers so that they can make seeds. Some flowers have brightly coloured **petals**, but many are dull green or yellow with no petals. Flowers have male parts and female parts. Sometimes they are in the same flower and sometimes they are in separate flowers.

The male part of a flower is called the **stamen**. The tiny grains of **pollen** are made in the **anther** which is held up on a stalk called the **filament**. The **anther** and the filament together are called the stamen. Flowers often have several stamens.

The female part of a flower has a sticky surface at the top, called the **stigma**. Pollen grains from other flowers stick to the stigma when the flower is pollinated. The **style** is a stalk leading down from the sticky stigma to the ovary below. The **ovules** (containing egg cells) are found are in the ovary. Together, the style, stigma and ovary are called the **carpel**.

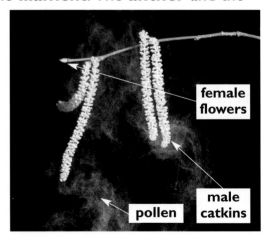

female flowers

pollen

male catkins

Hazel trees have separate male and female flowers but no petals; here we can see hazel catkins shedding their pollen

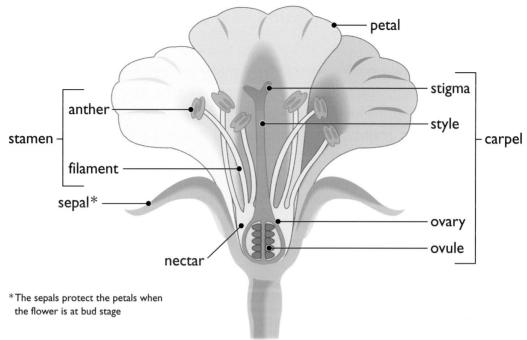

* The sepals protect the petals when
  the flower is at bud stage

Cross-section of an insect-pollinated flower

In order for the egg cells in the ovules to turn into seeds they must be
fertilised by joining with special cells from pollen grains. For this to happen,
pollen from another plant of the same species (type) must reach the flower.
The transfer of pollen from the anther of one flower to the stigma of another
is called **pollination**. Insects help to carry pollen to some plants. These
plants tend to have flowers with brightly coloured petals to attract the
insects. The flower may make a sweet liquid called **nectar**, which the insects
like to feed on. As an insect lands on the flower to
feed on the delicious nectar deep in the flower, its
legs and body brush against the anthers, and pollen
grains rub off onto the insect. The insect enjoys
the nectar, and so it flies off in search of another
flower like the first one to look for more. As it
lands upon the new flower and starts to feed,
some of the pollen grains on its body rub onto the
sticky stigma of this flower.

The pollen grains that are stuck onto the sticky
stigma in the flower now grow little tubes down
the centre of the style until they reach the ovary
below. Cells from the pollen grains join with the

The bee is covered in pollen

egg cells in the ovules and **fertilisation** takes place. The egg cells in the ovule can now grow to form seeds.

Plants such as stinging nettles, grasses and many trees do have flowers but they are not brightly coloured. These flowers need to be pollinated, but the wind does this instead of insects. Wind-pollinated flowers do not need to be colourful. The pollen grains of wind-pollinated flowers are very light and are easily blown by the wind. They must, however, land on another flower of the same type. For a pollen grain to land on the right type of flower takes a lot of luck, so many pollen grains will be wasted. That is why these flowers produce lots of pollen. The air in spring and summer is full of tiny pollen grains which often cause people to sneeze or suffer from hay fever.

To do: Flower hunt

Look around for flowers. Spring is a time when many trees have flowers so look carefully for them. Remember that the brightly coloured ones will be attracting insects and the dull ones you can hardly see will be relying on wind pollination.

Look carefully at the flowers you have found. Can you identify the anthers and the stigma in each flower? Decide whether each type of flower is insect-pollinated or wind-pollinated. You could try to draw a carefully labelled picture of each of the flowers that you find or maybe you have a camera that you can use to record what you have found.

If you want to pick a flower to have a closer look at it, remember to ask an adult if it is safe to do so and allowed (some plants are protected because they are endangered, so you mustn't pick them). Even if you can pick a flower, be careful not to damage the plant. Don't pick lots of flowers as they will never make seeds and so fewer new plants will grow.

Exercise 2.11

Use the words in the box to fill in the gaps in the sentences below. Each word may be used once, more than once, or not at all.

nectar	feed	petals	pollination	insects	pollen	anther
attract	wind					

1. Many plants have flowers with brightly coloured _____ .

2. The flowers are brightly coloured in order to _____ _____ .

3. The sweet liquid inside a flower is called _____ .

4. Pollen grains are made in the _____ .

5. The pollen grains need to be carried from flower to flower by _____ or the _____ . This is called _____ .

. . . .

Exercise 2.12

1. What is meant by the term 'pollination'?

2. Flowers may be pollinated by insects or by the wind. Describe the main differences between insect-pollinated and wind-pollinated flowers.

3. Which part of a flower makes pollen?

4. Explain in your own words how insects help to pollinate flowers.

5. Explain why dull flowers have such a lot of pollen.

6. Which part of the flower catches the pollen from the air or from the insect?

7. How do the special cells from the pollen grain get into the ovary?

8. What name is given to the process in which the cells from the pollen grain join together with the egg cells in the ovary?

9. What do the egg cells become after the process you have named in question 8 has occurred?

Exercise 2.13: Extension questions

1. Do you think that all nectar tastes the same? Explain your answer.

2. Make a collage picture or model of an insect-pollinated flower. Remember to show the petals, stamens (anther and filament) and carpel (stigma, style and ovary). You may even be able to put some ovules into your ovary.

. . . .

And back to where we started!

We have nearly come round in a full circle. We started with a seed germinating and growing into a new plant. The new plant grows and produces flowers. Pollination and fertilisation take place and seeds form. In order to complete the circle we now need to know what happens to the seed that is growing on the plant.

After fertilisation, the **ovary** swells at the base of the flower to form a **fruit** or **seed case** which often protects the seeds growing inside. The rest of the flower is no longer needed. Once it has done its job, it will wither and die. If you look carefully at a fruit (at the opposite side to the stalk), a banana or apple, for example, you can see the remains of where the flower has withered and dropped off.

The seeds need to spread away from the parent plant and find a new place to grow. This is called **dispersal**. They need space so they are not competing with the parent plant and each other for water, light and carbon dioxide, so finding a space of their own is important. Dispersal also makes it possible for plant species to move into and grow (colonise) in new areas. Can you think of any reasons why this is good for the plant species?

Using the wind to disperse seeds

Some seeds, for example orchid seeds, are very small and powdery and are carried away in the wind. Other seeds, such as thistle and dandelion seeds, are carried by a parachute that drifts in the wind and some, such as sycamore, have blades that make it spin like a helicopter in the wind. Some plants, such as

These dandelion seeds are being dispersed by the wind

poppies, have seed cases like pepper pots with little holes at the top. When the wind blows, the seeds are shaken out.

Using animals to disperse seeds

Some seed cases, such as burdock (see *Junior Science Book 1* page 112), have hooks that catch on animal fur. The seeds are carried away until they are scratched off. Some seeds are held in juicy fruits, such as blackberries and currants. Animals enjoy eating the fruits and the seeds are passed out in their droppings a little while later. Other seeds may be nibbled and destroyed by animals. However, some animals, for example a squirrel, may store nuts or acorns for winter food by burying them in the ground. Some of these will be left uneaten in the ground and may grow into new plants.

Some of the acorns buried by the squirrel will grow into new plants

Using water to disperse seeds

Water-dispersed seeds have waterproof seed cases that will float. These can drift for long distances across the sea and be washed up on a distant shore. Coconuts, some of the world's largest seeds, are dispersed this way.

Seed cases can even explode!

Seeds that grow in pods, such as gorse, often explode. As the pod dries, it twists and bursts open. The seeds inside can be flung out quite a long way away from the parent plant.

The witch hazel pod explodes spreading the seeds

To do: Looking at fruits

1. Make a collection of different fruits, and ask an adult to cut them in half so you can see the seeds clearly. Perhaps you could try a pepper, a tomato, an orange, a kiwi fruit, an avocado, or a strawberry.

2. Draw the pattern of the seeds carefully and label your picture.

3. Are all the seeds on the inside of the fruit? Are the seeds the same size? What differences do you notice between the fruits you draw?

To do: Sorting seeds

1. Collect as many different seeds as you can and try to sort them into groups. Start by sorting them into those dispersed by wind, those dispersed by animals and those dispersed by other methods.

2. Look at the wind-dispersed seeds and sort them according to how the wind spreads them about. Look for ones that are:

   (a) powdery and drift in the wind

   (b) spin to the ground

   (c) have parachutes.

3. Sort the animal dispersed seeds into:

   (a) juicy

   (b) hook onto animal fur

   (c) buried and forgotten.

Always remember, NEVER put seeds in your mouth, some may be poisonous to us (even though birds can eat them). Always wash your hands after any fieldwork.

To do: Make a flying seed case

Your teacher will give you a sweet to act as your seed for this challenge. You will also be given various materials to use.

Your challenge is to make a seed case that will keep your 'sweetie-seed' in the air as long as possible. Think about the seed cases that plants make for their seeds. You might want to model your seed case on one of these or maybe you will try something completely different.

When you have made your seed case, ask your teacher or another adult to help you try it out safely by dropping it from a height. How long does your seed case stay in the air? How far does it travel? Maybe you can compare your seed case with ones made by your friends? Which one works best? Can your explain why this one is better than the others?

Now the circle is complete!

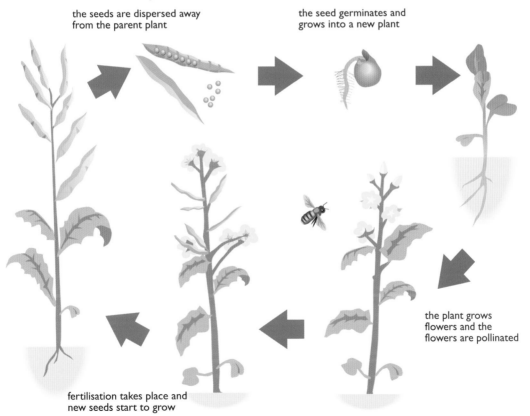

the seeds are dispersed away from the parent plant

the seed germinates and grows into a new plant

the plant grows flowers and the flowers are pollinated

fertilisation takes place and new seeds start to grow

We call this never-ending circle a **life cycle**. We shall learn about more life cycles in *Junior Science Book 3*.

To do: Cones

Conifer trees, such as pines, protect their seeds in a scaly cone. They come in many shapes and sizes. See if you can find some. When the seeds are ripe, and the weather is warm and dry, the scales will open and the seeds will flutter out. They will be carried and dispersed by the wind. If the weather is wet, the cone will close to protect the seeds.

If you place your fir cone in a warm, dry place the scales should open. Use a hand lens to look inside. Can you find any seeds? Place the cone in a damp place and the cone should close again!

Exercise 2.14

Use the words in the box, to fill in the gaps in the sentences below. Each word may be used once, more than once or not at all.

| disperse | wind | fruit | fertilisation | withers | flower |
| hooks | bury | waterproof | explode |

1. After _____ the ovary at the base of the _____ begins to swell.

2. When the flower has done its job, it _____ and drops off.

3. The seeds must _____ from the parent plant to find space to grow.

4. Seeds that are dispersed by the _____ often have wings or parachutes on their seed cases.

5. Some seeds have _____ so that they catch on the fur of animals.

6. Some birds and animals will _____ seeds to store them for the winter.

7. When a bird or animal eats a juicy _____ the seeds will be dispersed in its droppings.

8. A seed that is dispersed in water will need a _____ seed case.

9. Some seed pods twist as they dry and the seeds _____ from the pod.

Exercise 2.15

1. What does the term 'dispersal' mean?

2. Why is it important for plants to disperse their seeds?

3. Name a plant that uses the wind to disperse its seeds and describe how the seed case of this plant helps the seeds to disperse.

4. Why do some plants make juicy fruits around their seeds?

5. Explain how a squirrel may help an oak tree to disperse its seeds.

Chapter 3: Solids, liquids and gases

States of matter

Everything around us is made from materials that are in one of three states: **solid**, **liquid** or **gas**. We call these **states of matter**. You are probably quite good at recognising whether something is a solid, a liquid or a gas but have you ever thought about HOW you can tell? Sometimes it is quite hard to decide.

To do: Solid, liquid or gas?

Look at the pictures below. Discuss with your partner or group whether the material is a solid, a liquid or a gas. Try to say what it is about each one that helps you to decide.

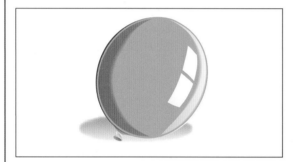

Air in a balloon

Log of wood

Milk

Ketchup

Did you find it easy to decide which state each of these materials is in? Was there one that was harder than the others? If so, why was it harder?

Properties of matter

When you were deciding whether materials were solids, liquids or gases, you were thinking about the ways in which materials behave. These are their **properties**. We learnt about the properties of individual materials in *Junior Science Book 1*. Now we need to think about the properties that groups of materials have in common. When deciding the state of a material there are two properties that are important:

● whether the material can **flow**

● whether the material can be squeezed

We also need to decide whether the material keeps its shape and its **volume** (size) if it is moved about.

To do: Investigating the properties of matter

For these activities you will need:

● 3 balloons:
  – 1 filled with air (a gas)
  – 1 filled with water (a liquid)
  – 1 filled with water and then frozen so it contains ice (a solid)

● sticky tape

● large bowl

● pin

● pair of scissors

Activity 1: Description snowball

1. Work with a partner. Observe and feel the three balloons and discuss the properties of the materials that are in them. Write down as many adjectives as you can to describe each one in the time your teacher sets. Remember that you are describing the materials in the balloons, not the balloons themselves.

2. Now join up with another pair and compare your words. Add to your list by writing the words that the other group thought of but you didn't. If you have time you can then join with another group of four and then maybe with another group of eight. How many good adjectives can the class think of to describe the materials?

Activity 2: Escaping materials

In this activity we are going to investigate whether each of the materials can flow, keep their shape and keep their volume (size).

1. Take two pieces of sticky tape, each about 5 cm long. Stick them onto the balloon containing air to make a cross shape. Make sure they are firmly stuck on.

2. Now take the pin and gently push it through the place where the two strips of tape cross. You should be able to make a small hole right through without popping the balloon.

3. Pull the pin out gently. Take it in turns to hold the back of your hand near the hole. Can you feel the air escaping? You might find it easier to feel if you make the back of your hand damp first.

Think about:

- Is the air able to flow?
- Where is the air going to?
- Has the air kept its shape? If not, what shape is it now?
- Has the air kept the same volume (size)?
- Do you think all gases would behave in this way?

4. Take the water balloon, put it in the bowl and use the scissors to cut off the knot. Watch what happens to the water when you let go of the balloon.

    Think about:

    - Is the water able to flow?
    - Where is the water going to?
    - Has the water kept its shape? If not, what shape is it now?
    - Has the water kept the same volume (size)?
    - Do you think all liquids would behave in this way?

    Remember to wipe up any spilt water, especially if it is on the floor.

5. Empty the water out of the bowl and put the ice balloon in the bowl. Carefully take the balloon off the ball of ice. You may find that it has already split but, if not, use the scissors carefully to remove it.

    Think about:

    - Is the ice able to flow?
    - Where is the ice going to?
    - Has the ice kept its shape? If not, what shape is it now?
    - Has the ice kept the same volume (size)?
    - Do you think all solids would behave in this way?

Activity 3: The big squeeze

You are going to find out whether solids, liquids and gases can be squeezed to make them smaller. If a material can be squeezed in this way, we say that it is **compressible**.

For this activity you will need:

- your ball of ice or an ice cube
- syringe
- water in a beaker
- bowl

1. Take the syringe and pull the plunger about half way out so that the syringe is about half full of air. Press your finger tightly onto the nozzle so no air can escape and then try to push the plunger back in.

   • Can you squeeze the air and make it smaller?

   • Is the air compressible?

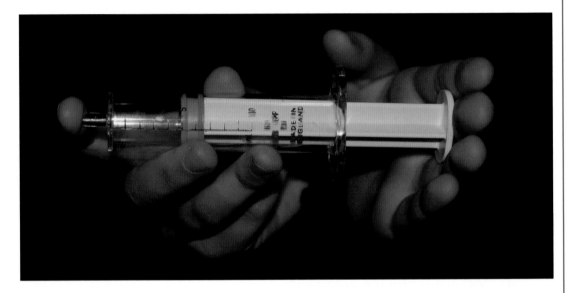

2. Take your finger off the end of the syringe and push the plunger right back in. Put the nozzle into the beaker of water and then pull the plunger slowly out until the syringe is about half full of water. Place your finger over the end again and hold the syringe over the bowl with the nozzle pointing downwards. Try to push the plunger in like you did with the air.

   • Can you squeeze the water and make it smaller?

   • Is the water compressible?

3. Push down on your ball of ice with your hand.

   • Can you squeeze it and make it smaller?

   • Is the ice compressible?

   Now you have done all these activities, you should be able to fill in a table like the one on the next page by writing 'yes' or 'no' into the spaces. You may be given a copy of it on a worksheet or you may need to copy it into your book first.

Property	Gas	Liquid	Solid
Can it flow?			
Does it keep its shape?			
Does it keep its volume (size)			
Is it compressible?			

Exercise 3.1

Use the words in the box to fill in the gaps in the sentences below. Each word may be used once, more than once or not at all.

liquid   gas   compressible   gases   liquids   volume   shape   solid   solids

1. The three states of matter are _____ , _____ and _____ .

2. If a material can be squeezed to make it smaller we describe it as _____ .

3. A _____ will keep its shape when moved about.

4. Both _____ and _____ can flow.

5. _____ spread out to fill the whole container or room.

6. A _____ takes the shape of the bottom of whatever container it is in.

7. Solids and liquids keep the same _____ when moved from one container to another.

To do: Mystery materials

Earlier you saw that it is sometimes difficult to tell whether something is a solid, a liquid or a gas. Here are three materials that will make you think.

Mystery 1: Sand

For this activity you will need:

- beaker of dry sand
- empty beaker
- syringe

1. Pour the dry sand from one beaker to the other. Does it flow? Does it keep its shape? Does it keep its volume?

2. Pull the plunger out of the syringe. Put your finger over the nozzle and pour sand in until the syringe is half full.

3. Push the plunger a little way in and then hold the syringe with the nozzle facing upwards and take your finger off the nozzle.

4. Carefully push the plunger in, pushing the sand up the syringe until all the air has been pushed out.

5. Put your finger back on the nozzle and try to compress the sand. Is it compressible?

Discuss:

- Is sand a solid or a liquid?
- Would it make any difference if the sand was wet?

Mystery 2: Cornflour

For this activity you will need:

- beaker containing some cornflour
- beaker containing water
- pipette
- stirring rod
- shallow dish or saucer

1.   Add water to the cornflour, a little at a time, using the pipette. You need to add just enough to make it wet but not so much that it becomes really sloppy.

2.   Observe the way the wet cornflour behaves when you stir it slowly and when you try to stir it quickly.

3.   Tip the beaker to allow the cornflour to flow out into the shallow dish then use your hands to form it into a ball. Place the ball in the dish and watch what happens.

Discuss:

●   Is wet cornflour a solid or a liquid?

Mystery 3: 'Slime'

Your teacher will give you a plastic bag containing some PVA glue mixed with water. You can add some food colouring if you like.

Your teacher will add some borax solution to the glue. You should then close the bag carefully and mix the two substances together until you see the 'slime' forming in the bag. You may need a little more borax to make all the glue turn into 'slime'. Pour away any watery liquid that remains and rinse the 'slime' under a tap or in a bowl of water.

Slime

You can experiment with your 'slime'. Does it flow? Does it keep its shape and its volume? You may find that you can bounce a 'slime' ball on the table.

Discuss:

●   Is 'slime' a solid or a liquid?

Remember to wash your hands after this activity.

Particles

All materials are made from very tiny **particles** (pieces) called atoms and molecules. These are so small that we cannot even see them with a microscope. However, the way they behave is important because scientists believe this is what gives solids, liquids and gases their properties.

If you could make yourself as tiny as the particles, the world would seem a very different place. You would not notice the

All materials are made from particles

things you see around you now because they would be so huge. Instead you would be surrounded by particles moving about.

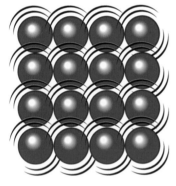

Particles in a solid are packed neatly together

If you were in a solid, you might see all the particles packed neatly together, like lots of oranges in a box. They would not be completely still. The particles in a solid jiggle (**vibrate**) as if they were shivering. They are quite tightly stuck together and cannot move around. This is why solids cannot change their shape and do not flow. As the particles are so close together they cannot be squeezed any closer, so the solid is not compressible.

If you were in a liquid, the particles would still be quite close together but they would not be so neatly packed. They would be vibrating more than in the solid and you might see them move around a bit. The particles in a liquid are not so strongly stuck together as the ones in a solid so they can change their places. This means that the liquid can flow and change its shape but the particles are still close together so they cannot be squeezed closer. The liquid is not compressible.

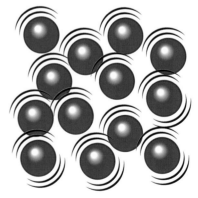

Particles in a liquid are not packed together neatly and can move around

In a gas the particles are not stuck together and are spaced widely apart. They have lots of **energy** so they are moving around fast in all directions and bumping into things. This means that they spread out and go anywhere they can.

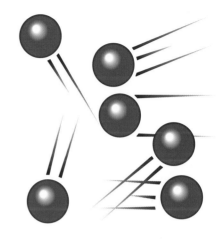

The spaces between the particles make it possible to squeeze a gas and bring the particles closer together. But the particles still have a lot of energy and so the gas pushes hard on the container it is in. For example, if the gas is compressed in a balloon, the energy makes a loud pop if the

Particles in a gas can move fast in all directions

balloon is punctured and the gas rushes out of the hole. We can use this energy to move things. The push of compressed gas can be so strong that it can be used to press the brakes on a heavy lorry hard enough to make it stop.

A gas (compressed air) is used to make the brakes work on a lorry

Exercise 3.2

1. Describe in your own words how scientists believe the particles are arranged in a solid.

2. Draw two diagrams to show the arrangement of particles in a liquid and a gas.

3. Use what you have learnt about the arrangement of particles in solids, liquids and gases to explain why gases can be compressed (squeezed) but liquids and solids cannot.

Exercise 3.3: Extension question

The first bicycles had wooden wheels with a strip of metal around them to stop them wearing out. Later bicycles had metal wheels and rubber tyres filled with air. Give as many reasons as you can why these later bicycle wheel designs are better than the old wooden ones.

Changes of state

Many materials can exist in more than one state. For example, water is usually a liquid but if you make it very cold, it becomes a solid, called ice:

Antarctic iceberg. The water has frozen and turned into ice

and if you heat it up it turns into a gas, called water **vapour**:

As water vapour cools it turns to tiny drops of liquid water that we can see and is called steam.

Water vapour is an invisible gas.

Electric kettle boiling: the water has been heated and turned into water vapour

It is easy to change the state of water by heating or cooling it. It is possible to change it from one state to another and back again. We describe these changes as **reversible**. The changes of state have special names.

Freezing and melting

If we take water or another liquid and cool it down enough, the particles become more neatly arranged and stick more closely together and the liquid turns into a solid. This change is called **freezing** (or sometimes **solidification**). To make a liquid material freeze completely, we have to cool it down to a special temperature called its **freezing point**. Different substances have different freezing points. The freezing point for water is 0 °C.

When we warm solids up, some of them will turn from solid to liquid. The particles become more energetic and they become less tightly stuck together. This change is called **melting**. Ice in a freezer is usually at a temperature of about ⁻20 °C. If we warm it up above 0 °C it will melt to form liquid water. We could say that 0 °C is also the **melting point** of water. Different solids melt at different temperatures. For example, chocolate melts at 37 °C. This is also the temperature of the human body and is why chocolate melts in our mouths so easily.

When water turns into a solid, we call the solid 'ice' but most materials do not have special names for their different states.

To do: Changing food

We can make some delicious treats by changing the state of some foods. Here are two recipes. Remember to wash your hands before working with food and use clean bowls and other kitchen equipment.

Recipe 1: Fruity snow

You will need:

- large bowl
- lots of ice
- salt
- plastic food bag
- plastic clip or twist/tie
- fruit juice
- spoon

1. Pour some fruit juice into the plastic bag and seal it up very carefully using the clip or twist/tie so that the juice cannot leak out.

2. Put lots of ice in the big bowl and sprinkle some salt over the ice.

3. Bury your bag of fruit juice in the salty ice and wait for it to freeze.

4. When it has frozen (possibly around 45 mins–1 hour) wipe the outside of the bag with a clean cloth, open it carefully and use the spoon to sample your fruity snow.

Recipe 2: Chocolate fruity cups

You will need:

- chocolate
- raisins or other dried fruit

- heatproof bowl
- large bowl or saucepan containing very hot water (Be very careful!)
- spoon
- paper cake cases

1. Break up the chocolate and put it in the heatproof bowl. (Don't eat it yet!)

2. Very carefully stand the bowl in the hot water.

3. Stir the chocolate carefully and the heat from the water will gradually melt all the chocolate. (Take care not to get any water into the melting chocolate.)

4. When the chocolate has melted, stir in the fruit.

5. Put spoonfuls of the mixture in the paper cases and wait for the chocolate to solidify. When the chocolate is hard, the fruity cups are ready to eat.

Did you know?
When water freezes it **expands** (which means it gets bigger). If water is left in a hosepipe in freezing conditions the water can burst the pipe as it turns into ice and expands. You might not notice this until you try to water your garden the next summer when the water leaks out through the split in the pipe.

Evaporation and condensation

Have you ever wondered what happens to the water in wet clothes when they are hung up to dry or where the water comes from when a window 'steams up'? These things happen because of water changing state from liquid to gas and back again.

When clothes have been washed, some of the water stays in the fabric and needs to be removed before we can wear the clothes again. There are two ways we can do this. We may use an electric tumble dryer, which blows warm air through the clothes, or we may hang the clothes up and wait for the water to disappear. But where does the water go?

Clothes will dry if hung on a washing line

The answer is that the liquid water in the clothes turns into the gas called water vapour. The water particles escape from the clothes and mix with the other gases in the air. This change, from a liquid to a gas, is called **evaporation**. Water can evaporate slowly at any temperature but it happens more quickly if you warm it up. This is why tumble dryers use warm air. If you make water hot enough, it will begin to **boil**. This means that bubbles of vapour (gas) start forming in the liquid water. They rise to the surface of the liquid and escape into the air. You will also see tiny droplets of very hot liquid in the air. We call this **steam**.

Liquids boil at different temperatures. We call these temperatures the **boiling point** of the liquid. The boiling point of water is 100 °C.

To do: Wash day

Mrs Mop is going to wash her clothes. She wants to know the best place to hang them to dry because she does not have a tumble dryer.

To help her, carry out an investigation to find out what conditions are needed to dry the clothes as quickly as possible. You do not need to use real clothes for your investigation. You can use small pieces of fabric or even kitchen cloths. Remember to make your investigation a fair test and think about how you will record and report your results.

Water vapour (gas) can get into the air in lots of ways. Every time you breathe out, you add water vapour to the air, because your breath is moist. Plants give out water from their leaves too. After rain, puddles evaporate and water is always evaporating from seas, lakes and rivers. We cannot see it, but there is always water vapour in the air.

If the air is cooled down, the particles in it slow down. Some of the water vapour in the air will turn into droplets of liquid as the particles begin to stick together. This is how clouds and fog are formed. This is also why windows become covered in droplets of water on a cold day. The cold air cools the window so that the water vapour in the air that is touching the window turns into water liquid. This change from gas or vapour into a liquid is called **condensation**. We often call the liquid on the window 'condensation' but this is not very scientific. We should say that it is droplets of water **caused by** condensation.

To do: Catch moisture from the air

You will need:

- glass or metal container

Put your glass or metal container into a freezer to make it really cold. When it is cold, take it out and leave it in a warm room, preferably one with people in it.

After a while you should see droplets of water forming on the container as the vapour in the air condenses onto the cold surface.

Did you know?
In the Namibian desert there is a type of beetle called the Namibian fog-basking beetle. It spends the hot dry days hunting for food, burying itself in the sand when it gets too hot. During the cool nights, it comes out and does a sort of handstand. Droplets of water from the night fog condense onto its back and roll down its shell into its mouth so it can have a drink.

Exercise 3.4

Use words from the box to complete the sentences below. Each word may be used once, more than once or not at all.

condensation	evaporates	freezing	condense	liquid
vapour	solid			

1. The change from liquid to solid is called _____ .

2. When we heat liquid water, it _____ to form water _____ .

3. When chocolate melts, it turns from a _____ to a _____ .

4. Water vapour in the air will _____ and form droplets of liquid on a cold window.

Exercise 3.5

1. Name the three states of matter.

2. How can you turn liquid water into a solid?

3. Is the change you have described in your answer to question 2 reversible or non-reversible? Explain your answer.

4. The change you have described happens at a temperature of 0 °C. What do we call this temperature?

5. What is the melting point of chocolate?

6. Why is it not a good idea to leave a hosepipe full of water lying in the garden all winter?

7. What name is given to the change from liquid to vapour (gas)?

8. If you heat water up enough, it will boil. What does this mean?

9. What is the boiling point of water?

10. What is the proper scientific meaning of the word 'condensation'?

. . . .

Exercise 3.6: Extension question

Explain, using your knowledge of the movement and arrangement of particles, why clothes dry more quickly on a sunny windy day than on a cool still day.

The water cycle

We have learnt that water is always evaporating into the air. We also know that, from time to time, it falls out of the air in the form of rain, sleet, snow or hail. The water is changing from liquid to vapour and back again all the time in a constant cycle called the **water cycle**.

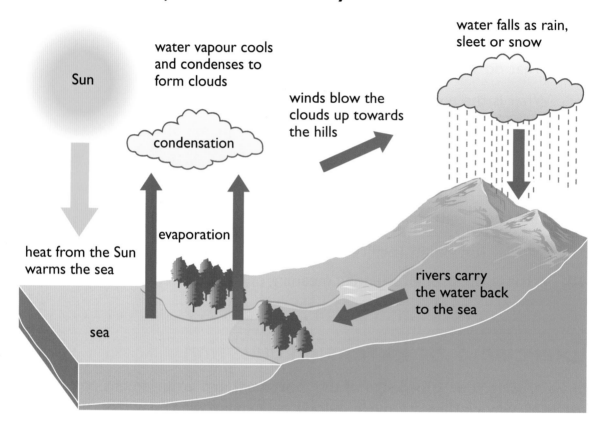

The water cycle

The heat from the Sun and the wind make water evaporate from the sea into the air as water vapour. As it rises and cools the water vapour condenses to form little droplets of liquid, making clouds. When the clouds are blown inland, they rise up over hills and mountains and become even cooler. The droplets of water get bigger and bigger and finally fall as rain. If it is really cold, the droplets might freeze and fall as snow or hail. The rain falls onto the earth and runs into rivers. The rivers carry the water back to the sea and so the cycle begins again.

To do: Make your own rain

You will need:

- large glass jar
- water
- cling film
- rubber band
- 2 or 3 cubes of ice sealed in a plastic bag

1. Put some water in the bottom of the jar.

2. Put cling film over the mouth of the jar and fasten it with the rubber band.

3. Make sure that the ice is sealed in the bag so that nothing can leak out and then place the bag carefully on top of the cling film.

4. If possible, put the jar in a warm place, for example in the sun, near a radiator or under a lamp.

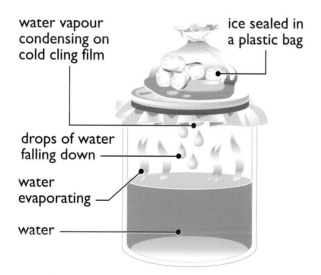

water vapour condensing on cold cling film

ice sealed in a plastic bag

drops of water falling down

water evaporating

water

Watch carefully and you should be able to spot droplets of water forming on the cling film where the ice has cooled it. When the droplets get big enough they will drop down forming 'rain' in your jam jar. You have made a little model of the water cycle.

Measuring temperature

Temperature is a measure of how hot or cold something is.

There are lots of times when we need to test how hot or cold something is. This might be as simple as deciding whether the weather is cold enough for us to need a coat when we go out, or testing the bath water to make sure that it is not too hot or too cold. The simplest measurer of temperature is our own body. We are quite good at simple temperature measurement, but it is not always reliable.

To do: Trick your body

You will need:

- bowl containing warm tap water
- bowl containing very cold water
- bowl containing room-temperature water

1. Put one of your hands in the warm water and one in the very cold water and hold them there for a minute.

2. Take your hand out of the cold water and put it in the room-temperature water. What does your hand tell you about the water?

3. Now take your hand out of the warm water and put it in the room-temperature water. What does this hand tell you about the water?

You probably found that your two hands were giving you different messages; one hand found the warm water quite hot and the other hand found it quite cool. This is because your 'body **thermometer**' does not measure the actual temperature of the water but compares it to the temperature of your body. This is why a room might feel very warm after you have been on a long, cold winter walk but chilly after you have been in a hot shower.

Over the centuries, people have tried to make devices to measure temperature accurately. An ancient Greek called Hero of Alexandria (10–70 AD) invented many things, including the first steam-powered device which showed that air expands when it gets warmer. He used this information to help him make a thermometer with water and air in a tube. As the air warmed up, it expanded and pushed the water level downwards.

Galileo, the well-known Italian astronomer, invented a thermometer that was made from glass bubbles containing liquid, floating in water. As the temperature changed, different bubbles rose or fell. These thermometers are still made today. Nowadays the bubbles usually have little tags attached showing the temperature in °C (degrees Celsius). In Galileo's day there was no scale to use and people invented their own scales. How confusing!

The first thermometers like the ones we know today were made in about 1654 in Italy. They contained alcohol, sealed in a tube, with a temperature scale on them. When the alcohol warmed up, it expanded and filled up more of the tube. When it cooled, it **contracted** and moved back down again. Still there was no standard scale so another famous astronomer, Dutchman Christiaan Huygens, suggested using the boiling and freezing points of water as the set points for a scale.

Galileo thermometer

The first scale to become widely used was set up by Daniel Gabriel Fahrenheit in 1724. Fahrenheit was a thermometer maker and was one of the first people to use mercury (a liquid metal) in thermometers. This made his instruments more accurate than most others. The **Fahrenheit** scale is still used today. On this scale water freezes at 32 °F and boils at 212 °F.

In 1742, a Swedish scientist, Anders Celsius, suggested a scale of 100 degrees (a 'centigrade' scale) with the freezing point of water at 0 °C (degrees **Celsius**) and the boiling point at 100 °C.

Scientists have invented many ways of measuring temperature, apart from the glass thermometer. You may have had your body temperature measured using a forehead thermometer containing special liquid crystals that change colour when they warm up. Electronic temperature measuring devices are also commonly used, for example in an oven or freezer. In school, you may have used a datalogger with a temperature probe. All of these use different

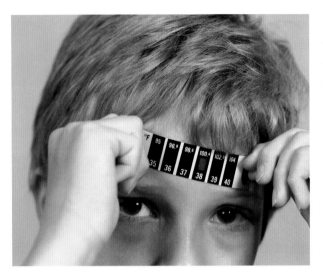

methods of measuring the temperature but people all over the world can understand what they are telling us because they all use the scale invented by Anders Celsius or the one invented by Daniel Fahrenheit.

Your temperature can be taken using a forehead thermometer

Reading thermometer scales

We can only get an accurate reading of the temperature from a thermometer if we read the scale properly. To do this we need to have our eyes level with the top of the liquid in the tube of the thermometer. We must then look carefully at the scale to read off the temperature. Here are some scales for you to practise on.

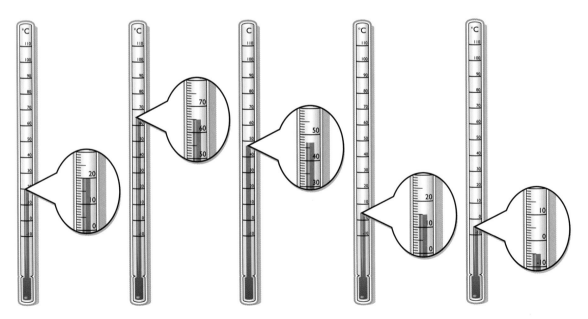

Check the readings on each of these thermometers

Exercise 3.7

1. What was the name of the Ancient Greek who invented an early type of thermometer?

2. How did Galileo's thermometer show changing temperature?

3. Why were early thermometers not very useful?

4. Glass thermometers work when a gas or liquid inside them expands and contracts. What do the words 'expand' and 'contract' mean?

5. Early Italian thermometers contained alcohol. What liquid was used inside the thermometer made by Daniel Fahrenheit?

6. On the Fahrenheit scale, what are the boiling and freezing points of water?

7. Name three places where you might find an electronic thermometer being used.

8. Why is it important to make sure your eye is level with the top of the liquid when reading a thermometer?

Chapter 4: Mixing and dissolving

In this chapter we are going to look at what happens when we mix things with water.

If you stir a little sugar into a cup of tea, the sugar seems to disappear. It can no longer be scooped out of the cup. However, when you drink the tea you can taste the sugar so it is still in the cup. What has happened to the sugar?

Like all materials, sugar crystals are made of particles. When the sugar is stirred into the tea, the crystals break apart and the sugar particles mix with the liquid tea particles. We say that the sugar has **dissolved**.

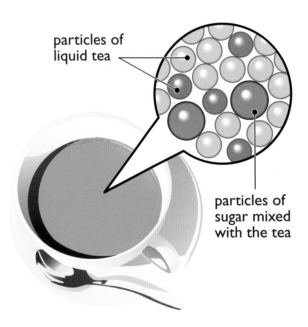

particles of liquid tea

particles of sugar mixed with the tea

The sugar dissolves in the tea

Substances like sugar that dissolve are described as **soluble**.

Not all materials are soluble. Some materials cannot dissolve and are described as **insoluble**. Sand, for example, is insoluble, which is just as well because otherwise it would dissolve into the sea and there would be no beach to make sand castles on!

To do: Soluble or insoluble?

You will need:

● beakers

● warm water

● spoon or a spatula

● stirring rod

Your teacher will give you some materials to test, for example, salt, pepper, flour, sawdust and wood shavings.

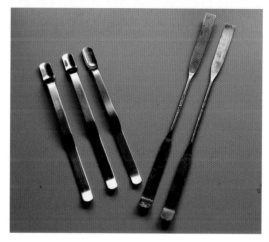

A spatula is a special scoop used in science

1. Half fill a beaker with water and add a little of one of the materials using the spoon or **spatula**. Then give the mixture a good long stir.

2. Look carefully at the mixture and describe clearly what you see.

3. Leave the mixture for a while and then take another look. Does it look any different? If so, describe what it looks like now.

If the mixture becomes a clear liquid, the material has dissolved and it is **soluble**.

If the material does not disappear the material is **insoluble**.

Sometimes the material is made from such tiny pieces they float around in the mixture for a while, making the mixture appear opaque or milky. This mixture is called a **suspension**. After a time the tiny pieces will drift down towards the bottom of the beaker and you will see them at the bottom of the beaker with clear water above. These substances are also **insoluble**.

Decide whether the materials you tested are soluble or insoluble.

Many of the key words you will come across in this chapter begin with the letter S. When a soluble substance dissolves, we call the mixture a **solution**.

A solution is made of two substances.

- The solid that dissolves is called the **solute**.
- The liquid it is dissolved in is called the **solvent**.

Solute (sugar) + solvent (water)   makes a solution (sugar syrup)

Exercise 4.1

Use the words in the box to complete the sentences below. Each word may be used once, more than once or not at all.

solute   solution   dissolved   cannot   soluble
solvent   insoluble

1. When a substance seems to disappear when mixed with water, we say that it has _____ .

2. A substance that is able to dissolve is described as a _____ substance.

3. An insoluble material is one that _____ dissolve.

4. When a substance dissolves in water, the mixture is called a
    _____ .

5. In a solution, the liquid part is called the _____ and the dissolved
    solid is called the _____ .

Making things dissolve more quickly

How can we make things dissolve more quickly? Discuss your ideas with
your partner or group. Here are some questions to help your discussion.

- When we put sugar in our tea, we always stir it. Does this make the
  sugar dissolve more quickly?
- Does sugar dissolve more quickly in hot or cold liquids?
- Sometimes people have special sugar with big crystals for putting into
  coffee. Does this sugar dissolve more quickly or more slowly than
  ordinary sugar?

To do: Sugar racing

The questions above mention three
variables (factors) that might affect how
quickly sugar dissolves:

- stirring
- the temperature of the water
- the size of the sugar crystals

Choose one of these variables (factors)
and plan an experiment to test
whether it affects how quickly sugar
dissolves. Remember to make your
investigation a fair test. Record your
results neatly in a table.

When you have all done your testing,
discuss the results with the rest of your class so that you all have the
answers to all the questions.

Exercise 4.2

1. Copper sulphate is a blue chemical that dissolves in water to make a blue solution. In copper sulphate solution, what is:

   (a) the solvent

   (b) the solute?

2. A scientist wishes to make a solution of copper sulphate quickly. Name three things she should do to help her do this.

3. What is a suspension?

4. Some pupils want to find out whether the temperature of the water affects how quickly copper sulphate crystals dissolve.

   (a) What is the one variable (factor) they should change in their investigation?

   (b) Which variables (factors) should they keep the same to make their test fair?

   (c) What pattern would you expect them to find in their results?

. . . .

Saturated solutions

You have learnt that a solution is made by dissolving a solute (soluble substance) into a solvent (such as water). If you go on adding more and more of the solute you will find, after a while, no more of the solute will dissolve, however much you stir. A solution like this, where no more solute will dissolve, is described as a **saturated solution**. Some substances, such as sugar, are very soluble and a lot of sugar must be added before you make a saturated solution. Other substances are less soluble and so less needs to be added before the solution is saturated. Examples of less soluble substances are salt and copper sulphate.

You have already found that substances will dissolve more quickly in hot water. Many substances are also more soluble in hot water so the quantity of solute needed to make a saturated solution may depend on the temperature of the solvent.

To do: Growing crystals

You will need:

- beaker containing 100 cm^3 hot water (Be very careful with the hot water!)
- another clean beaker
- fine copper sulphate crystals
- spatula
- stirring rod
- 1 larger copper sulphate crystal
- thread
- pencil or wooden splint
- safety glasses or goggles

Remember to wear eye protection all the time you are doing this experiment.

1. Add fine copper sulphate crystals to the hot water carefully, using the spatula.

2. Stir well after each addition to dissolve the crystals. You will notice that the colour of the solution becomes darker and darker.

3. When you are sure no more crystals will dissolve, leave the solution to cool to room temperature. Wash your hands thoroughly before you do anything else.

4. When it has cooled, pour the solution carefully into a clean beaker. You now have a saturated solution of copper sulphate.

5. Carefully tie the thread around the larger copper sulphate crystal and wrap the other end of the thread around the pencil or splint. (See illustration on page 76)

6. Balance the pencil or splint across the top of the beaker and adjust the length of the thread until the crystal is hanging in the solution and not touching the bottom of the beaker. This crystal is called a **seed crystal**.

7. Put the beaker in a safe place and then wash your hands before removing your eye protection.

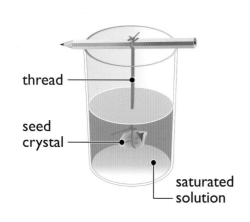

thread

seed crystal

saturated solution

Leave your solution for a week or two, checking it from time to time. Your crystal should grow bigger and bigger. This happens because the water in the solution slowly evaporates and so less and less copper sulphate can stay dissolved. The extra copper sulphate sticks to your crystal and makes it bigger.

What shape is your crystal? Is it the same shape as the ones made by other members of our class?

You might like to try making crystals of other substances, such as salt or sugar.

Exercise 4.3

Some pupils carried out an experiment to find out how the temperature of the water affects the amount of the solute needed to make a saturated solution. They did the experiment twice, using a different solute each time.

Here are their results:

Temperature of the water in °C	Quantity of solute that can be dissolved in 100 cm³ of water in grams	
	Solute A	Solute B
20	36.0	21.0
40	36.5	29.0
60	37.0	40.0
80	38.0	56.0

1. Describe how the temperature of the water affected the amount of Solute B that would dissolve in 100 cm^3 of water.

2. The pupils' teacher told them that the solubility of salt does not change very much with temperature. Which solute might have been salt?

3. Suggest how much of Solute A might dissolve in water at 100 °C.

4. Draw a bar chart to show the results for Solute B.

. . . .

Exercise 4.4: Extension question

1. On graph paper, use the data from Exercise 4.3 to draw a line graph to show both sets of results. Put **Temperature of water in °C** on the horizontal axis and **Quantity of solute in grams** on the vertical axis. Plot the points for Solute A first and then join them carefully with a smooth curve. Then plot the results for Solute B and join these points with another smooth curve. You might like to use a different coloured line for each solute. Remember to label the lines or use a key to show which line is which. Give your graph a suitable title.

2. Use your graph to find the following information:

   (a) At what temperature is the solubility of Solute A the same as Solute B?

   (b) How much of Solute B would you be able to dissolve in 100 cm^3 of water at a temperature of 30 °C?

   (c) At what temperature would you be able to dissolve 50 g of Solute B in 100 cm^3 of water?

3. Suggest how much of Solute A would dissolve in 200 cm^3 of water at a temperature of 60 °C.

Chapter 5: Keeping warm, keeping cool

Energetic heat?

Heat is a form of **energy** which we use for lots of everyday things. Can you think of five things you will do today where **heat** will be needed?

Heat energy does not stay still, given the chance it will move. It moves from warmer things to colder things and warms them up when it gets there.

To do: The same or different?

You will need:

- 200 cm³ of water from the fridge
- 200 cm³ of warm water
- **2 thermometers**

1. At the beginning of your lesson measure the **temperature** of both the water from the fridge and the warm water. Record the temperatures.

2. After 30 minutes, measure the temperature of both again. What do you notice?

3. Leave the water until the end of the day (or even tomorrow) and take the temperatures again. What do you notice now?

4. If you have another thermometer take the temperature of the room. What do you observe about all the temperatures?

Discuss with your partner or class what you found out. Why do you think it happened?

What do you think the temperature of the waters would be if they had been left outside on a cold day?

Heat will travel from a warm place to a cooler place until the temperatures are equal. Sometimes we want to try to stop heat from travelling. Can you think of any situations when we might want to keep heat in or out of something?

Exercise 5.1

Use the words in the box to fill the gaps in the sentences below. Each word may be used once, more than once or not at all.

| energy | warm | cooler | still | same | move | air | temperature |

1. Heat is a form of _____ .

2. Heat energy does not stay _____ ; given the chance it will
   _____ .

3. Heat energy moves from warm things to _____ things until they
   are both the _____ _____ .

Keeping warm

How many times have you been told to do your coat up and put your hat on because it is cold? Why do you think it can help you to keep warm?

Humans belong to the group of animals called **mammals**. Mammals are **warm-blooded**, which means they can keep their bodies warm using the energy they get from their food. The blood that is pumped around our bodies carries the heat that keeps us warm. Do you know what your normal body temperature is? If not, see if you can find a clinical thermometer and measure your body temperature.

'It's cold today. You must wrap up to keep warm.'

Heat travels from warmer to cooler places, and if we want to stay warm then we have to prevent our body heat from travelling away from our warm bodies into the cooler air around us. We put on clothes to keep the heat in, and in winter we put on lots of layers, especially if we are going outside. Other mammals have different ways to prevent their body heat from travelling away. Arctic foxes have very thick layers of under-fur and don't even start to shiver until the temperature is well below freezing. Whales and seals living in cold seawater don't have thick fur; but they do have very thick layers of fat beneath their skin, called blubber. Why do you think these marine mammals insulate themselves against the cold with a layer of fat inside their skin, whereas the foxes do so with a layer of fur outside their skin?

The process of trapping warmth is called **insulation**. We call materials that heat cannot travel through easily **thermal insulators**.

Keep it in!

There are many situations when we want to slow down heat loss. When we heat our houses in the winter, we want the heat to stay in the house and not escape into the garden. There are lots of different things that can be done to our houses to insulate them.

loft insulation

double glazed windows

curtains

lagging on hot water tank and pipes

cavity wall insulation

There are lots of things we can do to insulate our houses

Did you know?
About one-third of the heat in a house escapes through the roof if the attic is not insulated.

Insulation materials are often soft and fluffy. Can you think of any reasons why these sorts of materials might be good for insulation?

Think about the blankets or duvet on your bed. Why do you think they might be good for keeping you snug on a cold winter's night? Before people used duvets the same job was done by eiderdowns, so called because they were often filled with downy feathers from eider ducks.

To do: Which materials are best for insulation?

Try the following investigation to find out which material is best at slowing down heat loss.

You will need:

- several identical, empty, food cans
- different materials to wrap around the cans, such as aluminium foil, cling film, bubble wrap, thick knitted fabric, thin woven fabric
- warm water
- thermometer for each can

1. Collect various different types of material and wrap each one around one of the cans. Label each can with a number.

2. Look carefully at the materials and predict which one you think will be the best thermal insulator. Write down why you think this one will be best.

3. Now plan your investigation. How will you make your investigation a fair test? How will you tell which material is best at preventing heat from travelling away?

4. Put some warm water and a thermometer into each can.

5. Record the temperature on each thermometer when it stops rising (this will take about 30 seconds). Record the results carefully. Make sure you write down the correct temperature against each numbered can. Record your results carefully in a table.

Insulating material used	1st temperature, in °C	2nd temperature, in °C	Difference, in °C

6. After 30 minutes take the temperature of the water again and record these results.

7. By subtracting the second reading from the first you will be able to calculate the change of temperature in each can.

   Which material was the best insulator? Was your prediction correct?

A pocketful of air

Birds fluff out their feathers when it is really cold to trap air to keep them warm.

Feathers, loft insulation, fur and fibres are all good at trapping air. Trapped air is a good thermal insulator. Heat does not travel easily through trapped air so, if you want to stay warm, you need to make sure that your clothes trap lots of pockets of air. Woollen jumpers and jackets full of feathers trap air well. In really cold weather it is best to wear lots of thinner layers rather than one thick layer, so that you can trap more pockets of air in between each layer to prevent your body heat from travelling away. A duvet made from feathers or hollow fibres will help to keep you warm in the same way.

Mammals that live in cold climates have thick layers of fur to keep them warm. If you look closely at the skin on your arm, you will be able to see some very fine hairs. When we are cold, tiny muscles in the skin will pull these little hairs upright in order to trap the air in between them. We call these little bumps that stand up when the hairs are pulled upright in the cold, goose-pimples. Why don't we have thick fur to keep us warm?

Penguins in a huddle

In the Antarctic it can be very, very cold. Temperatures can drop to $-80\ °C$. Living in conditions such as these can be quite a challenge. The largest kind of penguins, Emperor Penguins, live and breed in the Antarctic close to the South Pole and are adapted to living in these very harsh conditions. A thick layer of fat under their skin and thousands of tiny feathers all over their bodies helps to insulate them from the air outside.

While it is still winter, the female penguin lays her egg, which she then passes to her mate. The male penguin carries the egg on his feet, covering it with a fold of skin, to insulate it from the cold ground and air. He does this for the next two months until the egg is ready to hatch.

While the males are looking after the eggs, the female penguins set off on a long journey to the ocean to feed. The male penguins do not feed at all in the two months when they are looking after the eggs. The winter storms rage and, in order to survive the extreme cold, the penguins gather together in groups of thousands to keep warm. They jostle and huddle in an enormous mass, moving like one gigantic animal, taking it in turns to be in the centre and then at the edge of the group. The penguins use each other to help insulate themselves from the cold winds and blizzards. They need to trap their own body heat and do so, not only with their own layers of fat and feathers, but also by using the bodies of all the other penguins in the group.

Penguins huddle together to keep warm

To do: Huddling penguins

Carry out an investigation to see if it really makes a difference where you stand in the huddle. Will the penguin at the centre of a huddle keep warmer than a penguin at the edge of a huddle? And what will happen if there is a penguin who is not allowed into the huddle?

You will need:
- 7 boiling tubes fixed together with a rubber band around them placed in a beaker (these represent the huddling penguins)
- 1 boiling tube in a separate beaker (to be a lonely penguin)
- container with some icy water (an ice cream box would be ideal)
- 3 thermometers
- warm water

1. Place your beakers with the huddle of 'penguins', and the 'lonely penguin' into the container of icy water.

2. Your teacher will have some warm water. Take the temperature of the water and record how hot it is. Your teacher will then fill each boiling tube half full with the warm water.

3. Place one thermometer in the tube at the centre of the huddle, one thermometer in a tube at the edge of the huddle and one thermometer in the lonely tube. Be very careful to place your thermometer carefully in the tube, it is easy to break the bottom of the tube if you are not gentle!

4. Now take the temperature of the water in each of the three tubes every 2 minutes for 24–30 minutes, and record your results.

What did you notice about the temperatures of the 'penguin' at the centre of your huddle and the 'penguin' at the edge of the huddle? Were they very different to the temperature of the 'lonely penguin'?

You could draw a bar chart showing the start and end temperatures for each penguin to show how much heat energy they lose.

Of course, these boiling tubes are not real penguins! How many reasons can you think of as to why this is not a true representation of real penguins standing in a huddle in the Antarctic?

Trapped!

In modern houses you will often see windows that are made with two or sometimes even three layers of glass. These sheets of glass are sealed around the edges and the air that is in between them is trapped and cannot move. Heat cannot travel easily across the trapped air, so the heat inside the house will touch the inside glass layer but will not be able to travel across to the outside layer and escape into the garden beyond! We call these windows double or triple glazed (depending on whether they have two or three layers of glass). They are very helpful in keeping our homes warm.

Some older houses cannot have **double-glazing** and just have a single pane of glass; it feels much colder inside these houses on a winter's day. Can you think what people used to do in order to try and keep the warmth from escaping through the windows?

Look around your home and school and see what sort of glazing has been used. You could draw a table and make a list of where you have seen single, double or triple glazing.

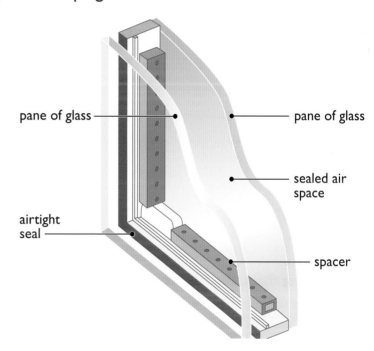

pane of glass

pane of glass

sealed air space

airtight seal

spacer

Double glazing helps keep our houses warm

When we go out for a walk on a cold day, we might take a hot drink with us. We could take some hot chocolate in a flask similar to the one invented in 1892 by a Scottish scientist called Sir James Dewar. A flask was made of two layers, one container inside a slightly larger container and the two were sealed at the top. The air in between the two layers was then sucked out to create a **vacuum** between them. The heat in the warm drink could not travel across the vacuum and could not escape, so the drink stayed warm for a much longer period of time.

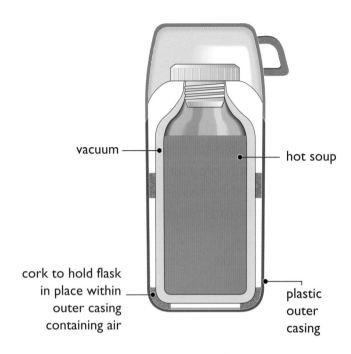

vacuum

hot soup

cork to hold flask in place within outer casing containing air

plastic outer casing

These early flasks were sometimes called Dewar flasks after their inventor James Dewar. In 1904 a German company called Thermos started to produce the flasks and nowadays when people talk about a flask they usually talk about a Thermos flask.

Thermos flasks keep drinks hot as the heat cannot escape across the vacuum

Exercise 5.2

Use the words in the box to fill the gaps in the sentences below. Each word may be used once, more than once or not at all.

| thermal | warm | fluffy | cold | insulation | pumped | air |

1. Mammals and birds are _____ blooded. Their blood is _____ around their bodies to keep them warm.

2. _____ keeps a house warmer for longer.

3. A _____ insulator is a material that does not allow heat to travel through it easily.

4. _____ is a good insulator.

5. Some insulating materials are _____ so that they trap air.

Exercise 5.3

1. Some insulating materials are soft and fluffy. Explain why these materials make good thermal insulators.

2. Look at the picture of the insulated house on page 80. Choose three places where insulation materials have been used. Explain why insulation in these places helps.

3. How do mammals and birds insulate themselves when it is cold?

4. Explain how a Thermos flask can slow down how quickly a hot drink cools on a cold day.

Exercise 5.4: Extension question

Imagine that you are a sales person for a double-glazing company. Design a leaflet to persuade new customers to exchange their old single windows for your new windows. Remember to explain how the double-glazed windows work to save energy and explain all the benefits. Try to think of a good name for your company.

The Earth in a blanket

The Earth is surrounded by a thick layer of air called the **atmosphere**. It is made up of a mixture of gases. The atmosphere acts like a huge blanket around the Earth, and helps to keep in some of the Sun's heat that is absorbed by the Earth. In the past this has been a good thing because this is how the Earth has become warm enough for humans and other forms of life to live here. Without the atmosphere insulating the Earth, the heat would escape back into space and the water on Earth would be frozen. For millions of years the atmosphere has been insulating the Earth and keeping it warm enough for living things to survive. This is called the **greenhouse effect**, and without it there would be no life on Earth as we know it.

Two important greenhouse gases

Two important greenhouse gases are **carbon dioxide** and **methane**. These gases occur naturally and have helped to keep the Earth's temperature steady for millions of years. However, people also make these gases in many ways and this may be changing our atmosphere in a harmful way.

We have already learnt that animals produce carbon dioxide when they breathe out, but carbon dioxide is also produced when fuels are burned. When we drive cars, fly aeroplanes and burn fossil fuels in factories or power stations, we are pumping millions of tonnes of extra carbon dioxide into the atmosphere. Trees and other green plants are absorbing carbon dioxide from the air, but humans are now producing more carbon dioxide than the plants can absorb, and to make matters worse many trees and forests are being cut down and destroyed.

Many human activities add extra greenhouse gases to the atmosphere.

Methane gas is also found naturally in the environment. It is produced in the digestive systems of cattle, and in the flooded fields where rice is grown. It is also produced when rubbish and waste material is rotting. The human population is growing, and therefore more cattle are needed to produce milk and meat. More people also produce more rubbish, as a result we are also producing more methane gas.

In the last 200 years, these gases that help to insulate the Earth have been increasing in the atmosphere and causing temperatures on Earth to rise. Scientists believe that the Earth will soon become so warm that some species of plant and animal may not survive. Scientists think that the temperature on Earth could rise by about 4 °C. This does not sound much but is enough to make a huge difference to life on Earth. This effect is called **global warming**.

Now that we understand how our lives have affected the atmosphere, and what some of the consequences might be, it is very important that we do all we can to reduce the amounts of greenhouse gases that are produced. We can all help by turning off lights and other electrical equipment, sharing car journeys, turning down the central heating and remembering to keep windows and doors closed. Can you think of more ways that energy can be saved, so that we put less of these greenhouse gases into the atmosphere?

Exercise 5.5

1. Name two greenhouse gases.

2. Explain how greenhouse gases make it possible for living things to survive on Earth.

3. What do scientists think is causing global warming?

4. Describe three ways in which you could help to reduce the extra carbon dioxide that is being produced by human activity.

Heat – Keep out!

So far in this chapter we have looked at heat travelling away. However, insulation materials are also useful when we want to keep cold things cold. To do this we need to prevent the surrounding warm air from travelling in and warming something up.

If you buy some ice cream at the supermarket on a warm summer's day, how are you going to get it home without it melting first? Discuss in your group what you might do.

To do: The ice dragon's egg

Imagine what you would do if one day you went to your freezer and found two huge frozen dragon's eggs inside. You want to take them to school to show your teacher, but wonder how are you going to keep them cold and stop them from melting.

You would need to find a material that you could wrap around your eggs. Would you choose a warm, woolly scarf or maybe a sheet of bubble wrap? What other materials might you choose? Share some ideas with your class. See if you can make some predictions as to which materials will work best.

When you have some ideas, ask your teacher if you can try some different materials to wrap around some 'dragon's eggs' (frozen water balloons). Perhaps you could divide your class into groups, and each group could try a different material. Remember that you must make your test as fair as possible.

You should also leave one 'dragon's egg' with no insulation material around it at all to see what happens if no insulation material is used. This will be your control.

When you have wrapped your eggs, leave them until the end of the day. How will you be able to tell which material has worked best? Where was the heat and where was it travelling? Think about how you will record your results clearly.

The ice dragon's egg

The heat energy, in fact, is all around you and the egg in the room, and even coming from the people in the room. The insulating material was reducing the amount of heat reaching the egg, so by wrapping the egg you were preventing all the surrounding warmth from getting to the egg and melting it. Think again about the 'warm', woolly scarf. Would the scarf make the egg warmer? No, it wouldn't! The scarf would prevent the heat in the room from getting through to the cold egg so it would keep the egg cold. A scarf only makes **you** feel warmer because it helps to prevent your body heat from getting away!

How to be a conductor!

So far in this chapter we have been thinking about how to slow down heat when it is moving, but sometimes we want heat to move.

When we put a saucepan containing water and frozen peas onto the heating ring of a cooker, we want the heat to move from the ring, through the base of the saucepan and into the water surrounding the peas as soon as possible. We want the heat to be able to move as easily as possible, so we use a saucepan made of a material that is a good **thermal conductor**.

When we do the ironing, we want the heat from the iron to move as easily as possible into the clothes, so the base of the iron is made of a material that is a good thermal conductor.

Can you think of any other situations when you would like heat energy to move easily?

Did you know?
When you pick up your knife and fork at lunchtime, they probably feel cold. Metal is a good thermal conductor; the metal is allowing the heat from your hand to move away quickly. So the metal feels cold to touch!

To do: Who goes first?

Try this experiment to see the difference between a conductor and an insulator.

You will need:

- 3 spoons the same size but made from different materials, e.g. metal, plastic, wood
- 3 raisins or peas
- 3 small blobs of butter or margarine
- beaker of hot water

1. Put a small blob of butter or margarine at one end of the lolly stick and the teaspoons.

2. Press a raisin or a pea onto each blob so that it sticks.

3. Place the other end of the lolly stick and teaspoons in a beaker of hot water and watch.

Which raisin or pea do you think will fall first?

Think about why the raisins or peas fell off. Which one fell first? Why did this one fall first? Describe what happened in your book or to your partner. Remember to use the terms 'thermal conductor' and 'thermal insulator' in your description.

Did you know?

Birds have very thin legs, and you may wonder how they manage to reduce the heat loss from their legs even when it is very cold.

The warm blood going down the legs passes very close to the colder blood that is returning from the bird's feet. Heat from the warm blood flowing downwards passes into the colder blood flowing upwards, and warms it. This means the blood going back into the body from the legs is not so cold, so the bird's body stays warmer.

Exercise 5.6

Use the words in the box to fill in the gaps in the sentences below. Each word may be used once, more than once or not at all.

plastic   thermal   insulator   metal   conductor

1. A material that allows heat to move easily through it is called a

    _____ _____ .

2. _____ allows heat to move through it easily.

3. Wood is a _____ _____ .

Exercise 5.7

1. Explain in your own words why a metal knife feels cold when you pick it up but a woolly scarf feels warm.

2. Imagine that you have met someone who has never seen a saucepan. Describe what a saucepan is like, which materials are used for the pan and for the handle and why.

3. Draw a picture of a kitchen and label it to show all the places where thermal conductors and thermal insulators are used.

Exercise 5.8: Extension questions

1. When people get lost in a snowstorm, they sometimes dig a hole in the snow to shelter in. Explain how this might help them to survive until help arrives.

2. People who live in hot countries often wear loose clothing. Explain how this helps them stay comfortable in hot weather.

Chapter 6: Electrical circuits

Electricity is a very useful kind of energy. We use electricity every day and would find our lives very different if we suddenly had to do without it. Have you ever had a power cut at home or at school? Think about what it was like. What could you *not* do while the electricity was off?

Static electricity

Long ago, people discovered that some materials make sparks when they are rubbed together. These sparks are an example of what we call **static electricity**. The word 'static' means 'staying still'. Static electricity stays still on an object unless it becomes possible for it to jump from one place to another, making a spark as it goes.

Lightning is really a huge spark of static electricity. Static electricity gives you those little shocks when you touch something that has been moving, like the handrail of an escalator or a car. As a moving object rubs against something else a static **charge** can be built up. This can then jump to your body when you put your hand near it.

There are two types of static charge: a '**positive**' (+) charge and a '**negative**' (−) charge. They behave a bit like the poles of magnets. Positive charges and negative charges are **attracted** to each other. Positive charges **repel** other positive charges and negative charges repel other negative charges. We can use this fact to play some fun games with static electricity.

To do: Games with static electricity

Fighting balloons

You have probably seen how a balloon that has been rubbed on a jumper will stick to the wall. Here's another trick with balloons.

Take two balloons, blow them up and tie threads onto the necks so that they can be hung up. Rub both balloons on a woolly jumper or on a cloth. It is best to rub both balloons with the same material for this trick.

Hold the threads and let the balloons hang downwards. Try to bring the balloons together. Can you explain why they push each other away?

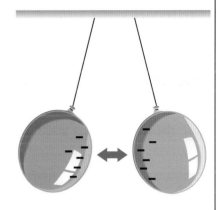

Fighting balloons

Obedient water

Take a balloon or a plastic ruler or comb and rub it on your jumper or cloth.

Turn on a cold tap and adjust it so there is a thin stream of water coming out. Hold the rubbed balloon, ruler or comb near the stream of water. What happens?

You will see a bigger effect if you do not put it too close to the tap.

Wake up sleepy Joe

Cut a sleepy Joe out of tissue paper, like the one in the picture. He needs to be about 6–8 cm tall. Make sure that your Joe has big feet!

Sleepy Joe

Use sticky tape to stick Joe's feet to a metal pie dish or a sheet of card covered in kitchen foil.

Rub your balloon, ruler or comb on your jumper or cloth again and hold it near Joe's head. Can you make Joe stand up?

Hair raising

This works best with a balloon because it is bigger than the ruler or comb.

Rub your balloon on your jumper or cloth to build up a good charge. Hold the balloon close to your partner's head. What happens to your partner's hair?

Let them try with your hair. Is there any difference? If so, can you think of any reason why?

A Van der Graaf generator makes a much bigger static charge than a balloon

Dancing cereal

Take a clean, dry plastic bottle. It must be very dry. Put a few pieces of puffed rice cereal in the bottle and screw on the cap.

Rub your balloon, ruler or comb on your jumper or cloth again and bring it near the bottle. What happens to the cereal grains? Try rubbing the bottle with your jumper or cloth to see what happens then. Can you think why this happened?

If you have some cereal hoops, tie a piece of cotton thread onto them and hang them up. You could ask someone to hold the thread, or you could use a small piece of sticky tape to stick the thread to the edge of the table. (Remember to ask first, as sticky tape can damage some furniture.)

Rub your balloon, ruler or comb and bring it near the hanging cereal hoop. What happens?

Exercise 6.1

Use the words in the box to complete the sentences below. Each word may be used once, more than once or not at all.

attract	north	repel	positive	static	negative	south

1. Electricity that stays still on a surface is called _____ electricity.

2. There are two types of static charge, called _____ and _____ charges.

3. Two surfaces with the same charge on them will _____ each other.

4. Two surfaces with the opposite charge on them will _____ each other.

Making electricity move

Static electricity is fun but not much use in everyday life. To make electricity useful, we need to make lots of it and make it move so it can carry its energy around to make things work. In 1792, an Italian scientist, Alessandro Volta, invented the first battery. It was a big pile of **metal** plates with wet sheets of card in between. He discovered that he could make the electricity from his battery flow along wires instead of making sparks.

Another important discovery was the electric light bulb. Two people, a British scientist called Joseph Swan and an American called Thomas Edison, both invented light bulbs at about the same time. No one really knows who had the idea first and the two men set up a company together to make their light bulbs. Some of these light bulbs were attached to Volta's batteries. A few years earlier another British scientist, Michael Faraday, had discovered how to make electricity using a magnet and a moving electrical conductor, which was a copper disc. The electrical current made by this apparatus was quite small. However, when the copper disc was replaced by a coil of wire, bigger currents could be produced and the first useful electrical generator was made. This made it possible to make lots of electricity. Edison improved Faraday's design and, in 1882, a street in New York became the first street to be lit with electricity.

Didcot, coal-fired power station; electricity is made in power stations

Electricity is now made in huge **power stations** but is still made using the same method. In most power stations, steam is used to make the generator work. Steam is usually made by burning coal or gas. These are called **fossil fuels** and they release carbon dioxide into the air as they burn. As we learnt in the last chapter, carbon dioxide is a greenhouse gas and scientists believe that rising levels of this gas in the atmosphere are causing **global warming**. If we can reduce the amount of electricity we use we can help to reduce our contribution to global warming as well as saving money.

To do: Help save the planet

Think about what you did yesterday. Make a list of all the activities that used electricity in some way. Now discuss ways in which you could have used less electricity. Maybe you could make a list of things that the whole school could do to use less electricity?

Design a poster to make people think about how much electricity they use and what they could do to use less.

Exercise 6.2

1. What must happen to make electricity useful?

2. What was the name of the Italian scientist who made the first battery?

3. Describe the battery made by the scientist you have named.

4. Who invented the electric light bulb?

5. Who discovered how to make electricity using a magnet and a moving electrical conductor?

6. Where was the first street to be lit by electric lights?

7. What is the name given to the fuels that are used in most power stations?

8. Why are these fuels harmful to the planet?

9. List three things that you have used today that need electricity to make them work.

10. Suggest two things you could do to reduce the amount of electricity you use.

Life without electricity

We are used to being able to switch electrical things on and off whenever we like; these might be lights, televisions, cookers and computers. For many people in the world this is not possible. In some places there is electricity for only a few hours each day and millions of people around the world have no electricity in their homes at all. Can you imagine what it would be like to live in one of those places? Emily is a student who visited a village in Africa. This is how she described some of the things she noticed.

'When I arrived in Africa, I was in a big city which was not so very different from cities in Europe. I did not stay there long and I soon set out on the long journey over bumpy roads to the village where I was going to work. We passed many small villages and I could see that life there was very different from the one I was used to.

At the school where I worked, we stayed in tents. There was no electricity. We had gas cookers to cook our meals and heat water for us. Luckily the weather was quite warm so we didn't need any heating. The children at the school came from the nearby villages and they lived without electricity, in small houses or huts. Their parents cooked on wood fires. They had no lights in the houses, although some had candles or paraffin lamps.

The children had no television to watch, no computer games to play and very few toys, but they were very happy. They played lots of games together and made good use of natural things around them to play with. Their mothers washed their clothes in the river and every child came to school looking clean and tidy.

Their parents grew vegetables to keep the family fed. Everything was fresh because there were no fridges or freezers to store food. In the school we had no computers and very few of the things that children in Britain have in their schools, such as books, art materials and sports equipment. All the children were keen to learn and worked hard.

It was a very different life in the African village. I missed some things from home but I soon saw that people can live very happily without electricity – just as my great-great-grandparents did in England.'

Many people in Africa still live without electricity

Making electricity work for us

How can we make electricity work for us? Let's start with a little challenge. You will use batteries because they are safer than mains electricity. You must never play around with mains electricity because it could kill you. The proper name for the thing we usually call a battery is a **cell**. This is the name we will use in this chapter.

To do: Light the lamp

Take a cell, two pieces of wire and a small lamp (light bulb).

Can you arrange these things to make the lamp glow?

How many different arrangements can you find that work?

Look carefully at the cell. It has two different-looking ends called **terminals**. The terminal with a little bump on the top is called the positive (+) terminal and the flat end is called the negative (–) terminal.

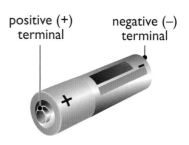
positive (+) terminal   negative (–) terminal

The lamps have two terminals too. One is the little metal button on the bottom and the other one is the screw thread. Look carefully at the lamp. Maybe your teacher will let you use a magnifying glass or hand lens. Can you see a very thin piece of wire inside? This is called the **filament**. When electricity flows through the filament, it gets very hot and glows. The filament is connected to the two terminals of the lamp.

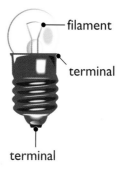
filament

terminal

terminal

To make the lamp light up, the terminals must be joined so a pathway is created for the electricity to flow round and round. This pathway is called a **circuit**.

To do: Make some circuits

Here are some pictures of circuits. Look at them carefully and see if you can make them using your apparatus. Your teacher will give you some lamps, cells and other **components** such as a motor or a buzzer, for example.

Be careful to make them exactly as shown. If your circuit starts to get hot, take it apart quickly. You may have made something called a **short circuit**. A short circuit is one where the electricity can rush around a path that does not go through any lamps, motors or buzzers. Because there is nothing to slow it down, it can go extremely fast. This makes the wires and the cell get hot.

It is not too dangerous when you are using cells, although you might get a little burn from it, but a short circuit in a mains circuit can cause fires or kill someone.

A

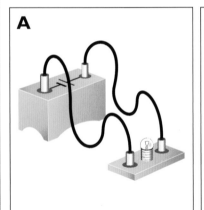

B

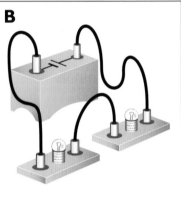

C

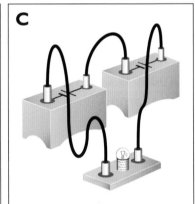

D

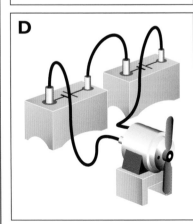

E

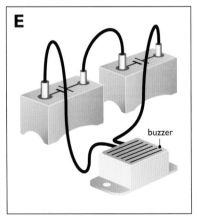

buzzer

F

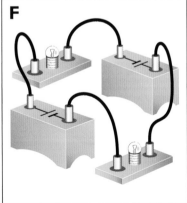

Why is it necessary to have a complete circuit?

Electrical energy is carried through a circuit by particles. The cell transfers energy to the particles and pushes them through the wires and components. If the cell is taken away the particles are no longer given energy and do not move around the circuit. If there is a break in the circuit the particles cannot go anywhere and so the energy is not delivered to the light bulb, buzzer or other component in the circuit where it can make things happen.

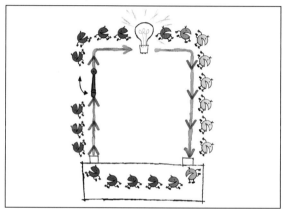

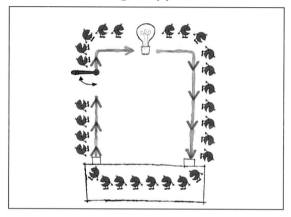

The particles carry electricity round the circuit

The particles have to stop if there is a break in the circuit

When there is only one path the electricity can take through all the components, we call it a **series circuit**.

. . . .

Exercise 6.3

1. What is the scientific name given to what we usually call a 'battery'?

2. Draw a diagram of a lamp and show where the terminals are placed.

3. How must the cell and lamp be connected to make the lamp work?

4. Why is it important for the components in a circuit to be connected correctly?

5. (a) What is a 'short circuit'?

    (b) Why are short circuits dangerous?

6. What name is given to a circuit where there is only one possible path for the electricity to take through all the components?

Conductors and insulators

In Chapter 5, we learnt about thermal insulators, materials that make it more difficult for heat to move. Some materials allow electricity to race through them but others do not. The ones that stop the flow of the electricity are called **electrical insulators**. The materials that allow electricity to flow through them are called **electrical conductors**.

To find out if a material is an electrical conductor or an electrical insulator, we can make a bridge of that material in a series circuit. If the material is a conductor, the electricity can flow through the bridge and the lamp will light. If the electricity cannot flow, the lamp will not light and so we will have discovered that the material is an electrical insulator.

To do: Conductors and insulators

1. Make a series circuit using a cell and a lamp, connected up with wires so that the lamp lights.

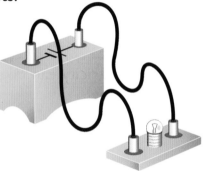

2. Now make a break in the circuit and add another wire as shown in the picture below.

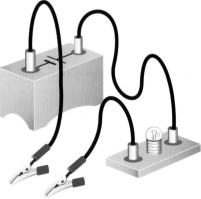

3. You now have a circuit with a break in it. Touch the ends of the wires together to check that your lamp still lights up.

4. To test your materials, place the end of one wire onto the material and then place the end of the other wire a little way away from the first one, making sure that the two wires are not touching each other. Look to see if the lamp lights up.

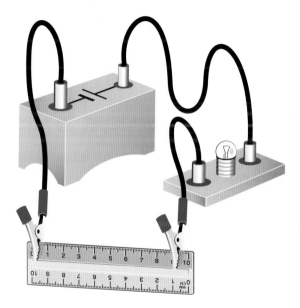

Try to test lots of different materials. A good one to try is the lead in your pencil. It is called 'lead' but it is really made from a material called **graphite**.

Record your results in a table with these headings:

Object	Made from	Does the lamp light?	Electrical conductor or electrical insulator?
e.g. wire	copper metal	yes	electrical conductor

Do you see a pattern in the results? Can you say which type of materials are electrical conductors? Are there any exceptions to this rule?

In the last activity you will have found that all **metals** are electrical conductors. **Non-metals**, except graphite, are electrical insulators. We need to use this information when we make electrical devices or components, such as switches.

Switches

Make a series circuit with a cell and a lamp as before but add a **switch** to the circuit. What does the switch do?

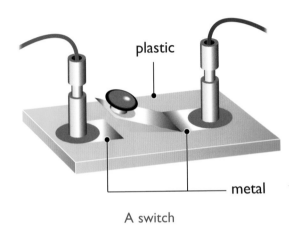

A switch

A switch is a device that opens and closes a gap in the circuit. When the gap is open, the electricity cannot flow so the circuit stops working. When the gap is closed, the circuit works because the electricity can flow through the closed switch.

Think about how your switch opens and closes that gap. Parts of a switch need to be made from materials that are electrical conductors and parts of the switch will be made from a material that is an electrical insulator. Can you work out where the conductors and insulators are on your switch? Do your ideas agree with your partner's?

To do: Make a switch

Your teacher will give you some materials. Some will be electrical conductors and some will be electrical insulators.

Use the materials to make a switch that you can connect into your circuit and use to switch the lamp on and off.

Draw a neat picture of your switch and label it to show where the electrical conductors and insulators are.

Exercise 6.4

Use the words in the box to complete the sentences below. Each word may be used once, more than once or not at all.

conductors	copper	graphite	steel	insulators	wood

1. Materials that allow electricity to flow through them are called electrical _____ .

2. Materials that stop the flow of electricity are called electrical _____ .

3. Examples of electrical conductors are _____ , _____ , and _____ .

Exercise 6.5

1. Describe how you would conduct a test to see if a material was a conductor or an insulator.

2. Michael says that only metals are electrical conductors. Becky says that some other materials conduct electricity too. Who is right? Explain your answer.

3. Draw a picture of a simple switch. Label it to show which parts are electrical conductors and which parts are electrical insulators.

Changing circuits

When you made your circuits you may have found that the lamps did not light very brightly. Can you suggest how they could be made to glow more brightly?

When we make one lamp glow using one cell, we call the brightness of the lamp '**normal brightness**'. In this exercise, we will describe the brightness of the lamps as being of normal brightness, a little brighter than normal brightness, much brighter than normal brightness or dimmer than normal brightness, etc.

To do: Bright or dim?

1. Make up your circuit with one lamp and one cell again. Look carefully at how brightly the lamp is glowing. This is 'normal brightness'.

2. Now add another cell into the circuit. What happens to the brightness of the lamp? What will happen if you add a third cell?

    Can you write a sentence saying how the number of cells affects the brightness of the lamp?

3. Now make a circuit with two cells and one lamp. How brightly is the lamp glowing? What happens if you add another lamp? Is the brightness of the lamps normal brightness, brighter than normal brightness or dimmer than normal brightness? What happens if you put a third lamp in the circuit?

Can you write a sentence saying how the number of lamps in a circuit affects the brightness of the lamps?

What do you think would happen to the lamp if you added a motor to the circuit with two cells and one lamp? If you have a motor, you could try it. Were you right?

Drawing circuit diagrams

Drawing pictures of circuits is quite difficult. We need to be able to draw a circuit, quickly and clearly, and in a way that everyone can understand. Scientists use special **symbols** to represent the parts of a circuit and draw **circuit diagrams** using these symbols.

Here are the symbols for the things you have been using in this chapter.

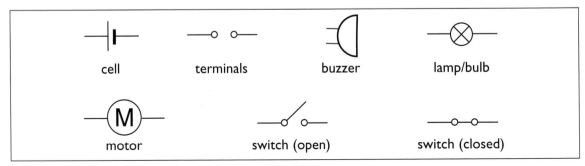

| cell | terminals | buzzer | lamp/bulb |
| motor | switch (open) | switch (closed) |

Circuit symbols

We draw circuit diagrams using a sharp pencil and a ruler. When we make circuits using bendy wires, they make bendy circuits. However, the bends don't make any difference to the way the circuit works. When we draw a circuit diagram we draw the wires using straight lines so that it looks neater.

Here is the circuit diagram for the first circuit we made, using one cell and one lamp in series.

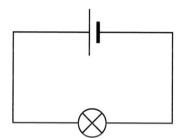

When we put a switch in the circuit, the diagram looks like this.

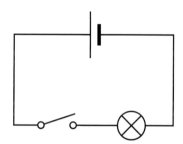

To do: Drawing and reading circuit diagrams

Using the symbols shown on the previous page, draw circuit diagrams for the circuits shown on page 102. The first one has been done for you.

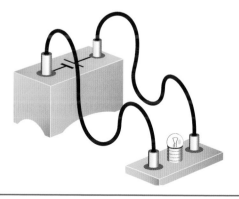 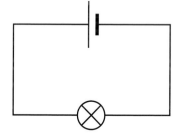

Here are some circuit diagrams. Can you make the circuit for each of them using your apparatus?

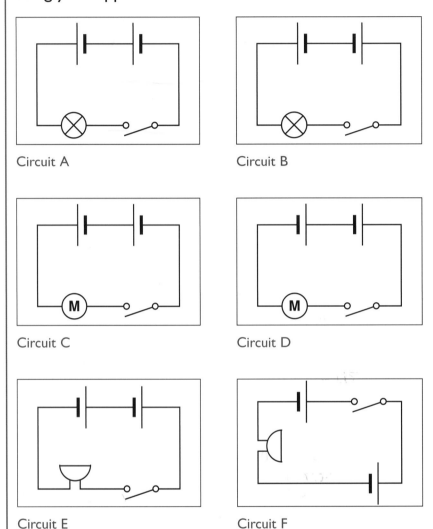

Circuit A

Circuit B

Circuit C

Circuit D

Circuit E

Circuit F

Can you identify the difference between circuits A and B?

What happens to the motor in circuit C when you change the cells round as in circuit D?

What is the difference between circuit E and circuit F? Does it make any difference to the how the buzzer works?

Now you know a bit more about how circuits work, you could make something with a circuit in it. Here are some ideas:

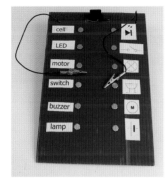

Game

Torch

How do you think the flowerbug can show which is its favourite flower?

Exercise 6.6

1. What are the circuit symbols for the following components?

   (a) cell   (c) motor   (e) buzzer

   (b) lamp   (d) switch

2. (a) Draw a neat circuit diagram to show a circuit with one cell and two lamps.

   (b) How brightly will these lamps be glowing? Explain your answer.

3. Some pupils have made a helicopter model. They want a circuit containing two cells and a motor to make the blades move round. They need to be able to turn the motor on and off. Draw a neat circuit diagram to show a circuit they could make.

Exercise 6.7: Extension question

Imagine that you are one of the millions of tiny particles that carry the electrical energy around a circuit. Think about what it might be like to move around the circuit, delivering the energy to the components. What might it be like in the cell?

Write a diary entry or draw a comic strip story to describe a day in your life as an electrical particle.

Chapter 7: Friction

What is friction?

Friction is a force that happens when two **surface**s rub together. Try rubbing your hands together. You should be able to feel your hands becoming warm. Friction often causes heat, but it can also cause the moving surfaces to become damaged and worn as they rub against each other.

Friction is sometimes known as **grip**. When you walk across the floor it is useful to have some grip between your feet and the floor otherwise you might slip over. Cars need to grip the road to stop them skidding. It is the friction between the two surfaces that makes them grip each other.

Friction can also slow things down. When you ride a bicycle and want to slow down, you pull on the brakes. This makes two rubber pads squeeze against the rim of each wheel. This causes friction between the pads and the moving wheel which slows down the bicycle.

Friction causes brakes on a bike to work

To do: Investigate which surfaces make the most friction

You will need:

● variety of surfaces (e.g. carpet, wood, paper, etc)

● small ball

Try rolling the ball across each of the surfaces in turn. What happens to the speed of the ball? Which surface do you think has the most effect?

Do you think what you have just done is a fair test of the surfaces? Think about how you made the ball move. Were you able to make the ball move in exactly the same way each time? What could you do to make the ball roll along the surfaces more fairly? You may need to ask for some more equipment to do this!

Plan a method for testing the surfaces in a fair way. Think about the things you need to keep the same to make it a fair test. What will you measure to get your results? How will you know which surface made the most friction?

When you have done your investigation, look at the surfaces again. Which property do you think affects the amount of friction created?

Rough and smooth

In your investigation you should have found that the **rougher** surfaces caused the most friction. **Smooth** surfaces create much less friction. Can you explain why this is?

When two rough surfaces rub against each other, the bumps and dips that make up the rough surface get caught up with each other, resisting movement. Smooth surfaces do not have such big bumps and dips so they can move past each other more smoothly, and therefore the friction force is less.

When we want to create more friction, we can make sure that the surfaces we use are rough. Think about the soles of your shoes and the tread on a car tyre. The patterns you see are there to create more friction so that the shoe or tyre grips the ground well.

In winter, we spread grit onto the roads. Ice on the roads makes the surface smooth so it is difficult for tyres to grip the road. The grit makes the surface rough again so cars do not skid as easily.

The tread on the tyre means there is more friction with the surface of the road or field

Exercise 7.1

Use the words in the box to complete the following sentences. Each word may be used once, more than once or not at all.

smooth   heat   rub   damage   rough   grip

1. Friction is made when surfaces ___rub___ together.

2. Friction can cause ___heat___ when surfaces rub together.

3. Friction can also ___damage___ moving surfaces.

4. Another name for friction is ___grip___ .

5. ___rough___ surfaces create a lot of friction.

Exercise 7.2

1. Explain what is meant by the word 'friction'.

2. How is friction caused?

3. Which types of surface create most friction?

4. Explain in your own words why these surfaces make so much friction.

5. Explain how spreading grit on the roads helps motorists to stay safe.

Measuring forces

The previous investigation measured the way in which friction affected the movement of the ball. The effect of friction was being measured, not the friction force itself.

Forces are measured in units called **newtons**. They are named after a famous English scientist called Sir Isaac Newton. When we measure things, we use a measuring device. If you measure the length of something, you use a ruler or a tape measure and measure in units such as centimetres. What would you use to measure the temperature of something? What units is temperature measured in? How would you find out how heavy something is?

To measure forces we use a **force meter**. These are sometimes called newton spring balances or newton meters. Force meters have a **scale** on them marked in newtons. If you lift a 1 kg weight using a force meter, you will find that it takes 10 newtons (10 N) to lift it. How many newtons would it take to lift 100 g?

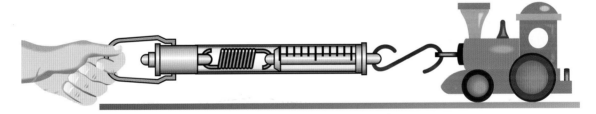

A force meter

There are many different types of force meter. Almost all of them have a spring inside them. The spring is carefully chosen so that it stretches by exactly the right amount when a force is applied to it. The scale on the force meter shows how much the spring is stretched by different forces. It is very important to use a force meter carefully. If you stretch the spring too much, it will not measure accurately any more.

Different force meters measure different ranges of force. You will probably use one that measures from 0 N to 10 N in most of your experiments but your school may also have ones that measure up to 20 N or 100 N. Make sure that you choose the right meter for the job.

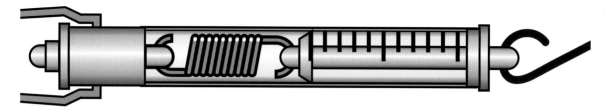

The spring inside the force meter is stretched by different forces

Some force meters measure pulling forces. These usually have a hook on the end to latch onto the thing you want to pull. Some measure pushing forces and these ones usually have a flat end to push with.

To do: Practise measuring forces

Your teacher will give you one or more force meters. Practise using them to do some pushing and pulling activities around the classroom. Make a neat table to record your results. Remember to write headings for the columns in the table and include units in the heading.

How many newtons does it take to push or pull the door open? How many newtons does it take to lift your school bag?

To read the scale accurately, make sure that you look at the scale with your eyes in line with the marker and read the value exactly. For example, it may take about 1 N to lift your pencil case but is that exactly 1 N or is it 0.8 N or maybe 1.1 N?

To do: Grippy shoes

Now you have learnt how to measure forces accurately, we can use this skill to investigate the grip of some shoes.

Measure the grip by using a force meter to pull or push the shoes across a surface. Place the shoe on the surface and pull or push gently. Measure the force when the shoe just begins to move. (You may need to try this several times to make sure you get the right answer.) This gives you a value for the grip or friction force between the shoe and the surface.

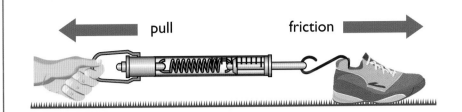

A force meter can be used to measure the grip of a shoe

Use this method to investigate one or more of the following questions.

- What happens to the grip if you make the shoe heavier by putting weights in?
- Which shoe has the best grip?
- Does the size of the shoe make any difference?

Don't forget to make your investigations as fair as possible.

Record your measurements neatly in a table and explain your results using your knowledge of friction and forces.

Maybe you can think of other questions to investigate if you have time.

Exercise 7.3

Use the words in the box to complete the following sentences. Each word may be used once, more than once or not at all.

| newtons centimetres accurately stretched |
| force meter ruler |

1. We can measure forces using a _force meter_.

2. Forces are measured using units called _newtons_.

3. Force meters must not be _streched_ too much or they will stop measuring _accurately_.

Exercise 7.4

1. Some pupils are given three blocks of wood. One has sandpaper on the bottom, one has carpet on the bottom and the third has shiny plastic on the bottom. Each block has a small hook on the side so it can be pulled across the table.

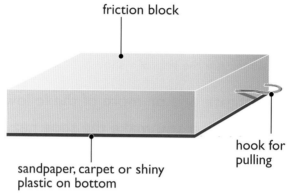

friction block

hook for pulling

sandpaper, carpet or shiny plastic on bottom

(a) Describe clearly how they could measure the friction force between one of the blocks and the table.

(b) The pupils want to find out which block caused the most friction. What should they keep the same to make their test fair?

(c) Which surface do you predict would cause the most friction? Explain your answer.

2. The pupils then repeated their test but this time they placed some weights on top of the block. Do you think that their friction measurements would be lower, the same or higher, than in their first test? Explain your answer.

. . . .

Exercise 7.5: Extension question

Look at the experiment described in Exercise 7.4. Here is how Claire reported her findings.

'I pulled the blocks and I found that the shiny plastic one took 3.1 N to pull it. The sandpaper one took 2.4 N and the carpet one took 3.4 N. I thought the sandpaper would make the most friction. James got different results from me. He got 0.8 N for the plastic, 2.1 N for the sandpaper and 3.2 N for the carpet.'

(a) Do you think that James or Claire had carried out the experiment more carefully? Explain your answer.

(b) When Claire and James compared their results, they found they were different. What would you suggest they should do about this?

(c) Draw a bar chart to show James's results for this experiment.

Friction – friend or foe?

Whilst it is useful that shoes have grippy soles, friction is not always so welcome. If you go skiing, you want to be able to slide smoothly down the slope. If there was a lot of friction between the snow and the skis, you wouldn't go very fast at all and that would be no fun. What would it be like if a playground slide had a rough surface?

Look at the pictures below. In each picture, there are surfaces moving past each other. Discuss whether you think friction is being helpful or a nuisance in each case.

Reducing friction

When friction is a nuisance, we want to reduce the friction force as much as possible. Earlier in the chapter you found that rough surfaces create a lot of friction and smoother ones allow the surfaces to slide past each other more easily. To reduce the friction force we need to make the rubbing surfaces move as smoothly as possible.

We can do this by making the surfaces very smooth. The bottom of an ice skate, for example, is made from shiny, smooth metal so it glides easily over the smooth ice.

It is also possible to reduce friction by putting something slippery, like oil, in between the rubbing surfaces. Try rubbing your hands together, as we did at the beginning of the chapter. Now put some water and soap on your hands. Don't use too much soap or it will get sticky rather than slippery! Rub your hands together again. Can you feel how the slippery soap is helping your hands to slide past each other? A slippery liquid, such as oil, that is used to help things move smoothly is called a **lubricant**.

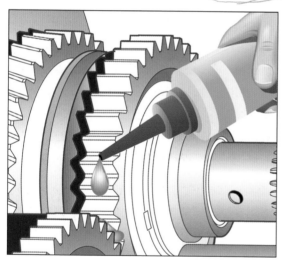

Oil is used as a lubricant

Moving parts in cars, bicycles and factory machines are kept moving smoothly by using lubricants. This also protects the surfaces of the parts from becoming damaged. If we find that door hinges start to rub together and become hard to move, a little oil will make them move smoothly again. The vibration caused by the rubbing hinges sometimes makes a squeaky noise. Oiling makes them quiet again. Can you think of any other places where a little oil might help things to move smoothly?

Another way to make things move smoothly is to use little metal balls called ball bearings. The ball bearings are placed between the two parts and when the parts start to move, they roll along helping the surfaces of the parts to move over each other without rubbing together.

Air and water

When cars, lorries, planes, birds and other moving objects move through the air, they are, in fact, rubbing against the tiny air particles that make up the air. It seems strange that something like air can cause friction but it happens because the air particles have to move out of the way of the object. The friction caused by the air is called **air resistance**.

To do: Feel air resistance

You will need a large piece of stiff card or board.
Go outside to do this experiment, if you can.

Start running without the card or board. Can you feel the air pushing against you? What does it feel like?

Now take the piece of card or board and hold it upright in front of you. When you run this time there is a much bigger surface for the air to rub against. What does it feel like now?

When we want to make something move very fast, we have to think about reducing this kind of friction force. We can do this by changing the shape of the moving object so the air can flow past it smoothly. We call this **streamlining**. Think about the shape of an aeroplane or a racing car. They have pointed fronts and smooth shapes. The air is pushed out of the way by the pointed nose and then flows smoothly along the body of the vehicle.

Can you explain why racing cyclists have strange shaped helmets?

When spacecraft return to Earth they come through the atmosphere and travel extremely fast. The air resistance is enormous. When something travels as fast as this through air, it will get very hot because friction causes heat. Spacecraft have to be very well insulated to stop them burning up. Space rocks that enter the atmosphere get very hot too. Small ones burn up as they race through the air. We call these meteors or shooting stars.

Boats, and other things that move through water, also move more easily because they are streamlined. Think about the shape of a dolphin. Its pointed nose and smooth body are the perfect shape for shooting through the water (and air) at high speed.

Dolphins are streamlined so that they can shoot through the water and the air

To do: Sinking shapes

This is a very sticky experiment! Take care not to make too much mess. Clear up any spills immediately and remember to wash your hands after doing your experiment.

You will need:

- deep container made of glass or clear plastic filled with wallpaper paste
- modelling clay
- timer or stopwatch

1. Divide the clay into six equal-sized shapes. Roll one shape into a ball. Make one piece into a bullet shape, make one into a short fat cylinder with flat ends and then make the fourth piece into an interesting shape of your choice. Make sure that your shapes can fit into the container of paste. Keep the other two pieces on one side for now.

2. Make a mark on the container near the top of the paste and another near the bottom.

3. Drop each shape into the paste in turn. Start the timer when it reaches the upper mark and stop it when it reaches the lower one. Compare the times taken for the shapes to drop through the paste. Which shape dropped the quickest? Which took longest to fall? Can you explain why?

4. With your last two pieces of modelling clay, see if you can make another shape that you think will drop faster than your fastest one from the first test. Can you make one that will go even slower than your slowest one?

Explain to your partner or group why you have made your shapes this way before you try them out. Can your partner suggest any way of improving your design?

Now test them. Were you successful?

Exercise 7.6

Use the words in the box to complete the following sentences. Each word may be used once, more than once or not at all.

streamlined	helpful	lubricants	heat	smooth
nuisance	atmosphere	fat		

1. Friction can be __helpful__ or a __nuisance__.

2. We can reduce friction by making the surface of the moving parts very __smooth__.

3. Oil and other liquids that make the surface of the moving parts slippery are called __lubricants__

4. A __streamlined__ shape moves more smoothly through air or water.

5. Space rocks that enter the Earth's __atmosphere__ burn up because of __heat__ caused by friction. They are seen as shooting stars.

6. A dolphin has a very __smooth__ body so that it can move quickly through the water.

Exercise 7.7

1. Give three examples of situations, apart from grip on shoes and tyres, where friction is helpful.

2. Give three examples of situations where friction is a nuisance.

3. Explain why you might put oil on a squeaky door hinge.

4. (a) What name is given to the friction force made when things move through the air?

   (b) How can this friction force be reduced?

5. Why do spacecraft returning to Earth have to be very well insulated?

6. What is a shooting star?

7. Suggest a reason why submarines have a similar shape to a whale.

Exercise 7.8: Extension question

Sharks have narrow bodies, smooth skins and pointed noses. Puffer fish are rounded and have rough spiny skins. What do these facts suggest about the lifestyles of these two fish? Give as many reasons as you can for the differences between the two.

Ancient builders

Over 4000 years ago in Wiltshire in the south of England people started to build Stonehenge. Stonehenge was formed from a circle of massive stone arches, and an inner circle of smaller stones. No one knows exactly why it was built. It may have been a kind of temple, or a huge sundial, or a place to observe the movement of the stars and planets.

Stonehenge

The stones of the inner circle may not be the largest, but they still weigh about 4 tonnes each. They came from the Preseli mountains in Wales, about 240 miles away. Transporting such large stones over this distance would have been quite a large undertaking.

Over 500 men would have been needed to move each stone at Stonehenge

We do not know for certain how the stones were moved. It is likely that for some of the journey they would have been put on barges and floated along a river. Even so, they would have been moved overland for long distances. The wheel hadn't been invented by the time Stonehenge was built. Many historians believe the stones were placed on rollers, probably whole tree trunks, and pulled along using leather ropes. As the stones moved across the rollers, the roller at the back would roll out from under the stone. Men would carry it to the front of the stone and then pull the stone onto it, releasing the next one from the back. What a lot of work!

The outer circle is made of even bigger stones, up to 50 tonnes each. These came from much nearer the site but they are far too heavy to have been taken by river. They would have sunk the boat! These ones must have come overland. Some people have calculated that it would have taken 500 men pulling on leather ropes to move each stone and another 100 men to move the rollers.

Somehow these massive stones were tipped up on end and settled into pits in the ground to make the stone circle. Large stones, or lintels, were then heaved up and placed across the top. Although Stonehenge was built thousands of years ago, the ancient people who built it obviously knew a lot about forces and especially about how to overcome friction forces!

Exercise 7.9

1. Where is Stonehenge?

2. When did the building of Stonehenge begin?

3. How far did the stones for the inner ring have to be transported?

4. How heavy are the largest stones in the outer ring of Stonehenge?

5. Explain, using your knowledge of forces, why the builders of Stonehenge would have found it difficult to move these stones.

6. Describe in your own words how historians believe these huge stones might have been transported.

7. Explain why this method would make it easier to move the stones.

8. What other method was probably used for moving some of the stones?

9. Why was it not possible to use this method for all the stones?

10. What do historians believe Stonehenge might have been used for?

To do: Rollers

You will need:

- book
- some string to tie around the book if you are using a pulling force meter
- lots of round pencils or lengths of dowelling
- force meter

1. Place the book on the table and push or pull it to measure the friction force.

2. Put the round pencils or dowelling on the table and put the book on top.

3. Push or pull the book gently across the rollers and measure the force.

Can you see how the stones for Stonehenge could be moved in this way?

Chapter 8: Sun, Earth and Moon

When we look up into a cloudless night sky, we can often see a beautiful collection of bright **stars**. There are many millions of stars in the **universe**, all grouped together into clusters called **galaxies**. The stars we can see in the night sky are the ones in our own galaxy, the **Milky Way**.

All over the world, for thousands of years, people have looked up into the sky and tried to make sense of what they could see. In many places, ancient peoples worshipped things they could see in the sky. Some believed that the Sun was a god, some worshipped the **Moon**. People often saw patterns in the stars and used these to forecast the future.

The Inca people of Peru worshipped the Sun

We still pick out patterns in the stars to help us to find our way around the night sky. These patterns are called **constellations**. Maybe you can recognise some. The best known are the Great Bear (sometimes called the saucepan or big dipper) and Orion the hunter.

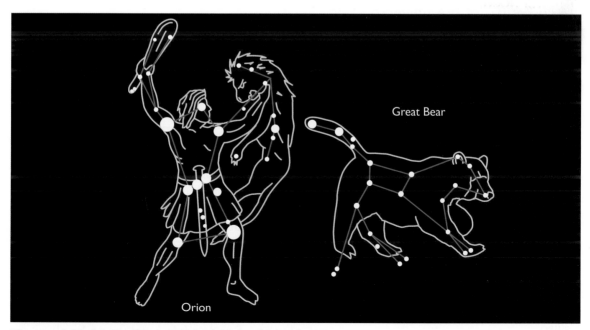

Great Bear

Orion

The Great Bear and Orion constellations

To do: Constellations

1. Use books or the internet to find the patterns of stars that make up some of the constellations. You could start by finding out about Cassiopeia, Draco and the Southern Cross. You could make the patterns by sticking silver stars onto black paper for a display.

2. Look at a newspaper, the internet or a magazine to find out about the night sky you could see tonight. Where will you look to find the North Star? Which constellations will be visible? Will you be able to see any of the **planets**?

People who study the universe are called **astronomers**. Early astronomers had to rely on what they could see with their naked eyes. Until the 16th century, people believed that the Earth was at the centre of the Universe and that everything else moved around it. In 1530, an astronomer called Copernicus published a book explaining that the Earth was one of a number of planets that **orbit** the Sun. This idea was not completely new because a number of thinkers had suggested it earlier, but the idea had never been fully accepted. Another scientist, Galileo (1564–1642), also believed that the Earth moved round the Sun. He got into a lot of trouble with the leaders of the Roman Catholic Church who believed that the Bible said that the Earth was at the centre of the universe.

Galileo

Galileo was probably the first person to observe the stars and planets using a **telescope**. He made his own telescope, which was not at all powerful by today's standards, but it let him see the planets in more detail. He was the first person to identify some of Jupiter's moons.

Nowadays we have telescopes that are much more powerful. Some are massive, some are out in space, orbiting (going round and round) the Earth. They allow us to see out into space, beyond the Milky Way, and to find out about distant stars and planets. Spacecraft have sent back

pictures of the planets and their moons. Some people have even left the Earth and travelled to the Moon. All these things have helped us to find out more about the universe and especially our nearest neighbours in the solar system.

Man landing on the Moon

To do: Space missions

Find out about some of the spacecraft that have been launched from Earth and where they have visited. See if you can find any pictures they have sent back to Earth. You might like to start with Cassini, the Venus Express, some of the Apollo missions or the Hubble telescope.

Exercise 8.1

Use the words in the box to fill in the gaps in the sentences below. Each word may be used once, more than once or not at all.

Moon telescopes spacecraft galaxies astronomer constellations stars planets Milky Way Galileo

1. The universe contains millions of _____ grouped together into clusters called _____ .

2. Our galaxy is called the _____ .

3. People often look for patterns in the stars. We call these patterns _____ .

4. A scientist who studies the universe is called an _____ .

5. Early astronomers could not see many of the planets because they did not have _____ to look through.

6. _____ was the first astronomer to identify some of the moons of Jupiter.

7. The furthest that any person has travelled from Earth is to the _____ .

. . . .

The solar system

The **Sun** is a star. It is a huge ball of burning gas and is incredibly hot. It is about 15 million degrees Celsius at the centre. The Sun is about 150 million kilometres away from the Earth. The heat from the Sun that reaches the Earth makes it a good place to live.

Did you know?
Light travels so fast that it only takes 8½ minutes to travel the 150 million kilometres from the Sun to the Earth!

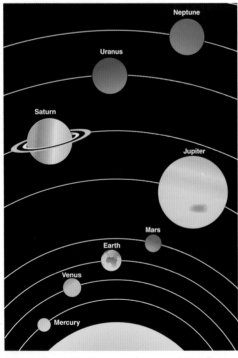
The solar system

Orbiting the Sun are the planets. There are eight planets in our solar system, all named after gods and people from mythology, apart from the Earth. Planets are all spherical (ball-shaped), some are made from rocks and some are made from gas. They all travel around the Sun because the Sun's **gravity** pulls on them and stops them escaping into space. If we could travel from the Sun into the solar system, visiting the planets in turn, what would we see?

The planet nearest the Sun is called **Mercury**. The Romans believed that Mercury was the messenger to their gods. Mercury is a rocky planet that gets amazingly hot in the daytime (about 350 °C) and extremely cold at night (−178 °C).

After Mercury comes **Venus**. Venus was the Roman goddess of beauty but the planet Venus would not be a beautiful place to live. It is very hot and has thick acidic clouds and very strong winds. One spacecraft landed on Venus but only managed to send messages back to Earth for less than an hour before its instruments were quickly destroyed by the heat.

The third planet from the Sun is **Earth**. As far as we know, Earth is the only place in the solar system where life exists. This is because living things need water. Earth is the only place where the temperature is not so hot that water boils away or so cold that it is all frozen solid. Maybe we will find life somewhere else, either in our solar system or on a planet orbiting another star somewhere in the Universe.

Planet number four is **Mars**, named after the Roman god of war. Mars is sometimes called the Red Planet because its surface is covered with red dust and rocks. We know a lot about Mars because many space probes have visited it and taken pictures of it.

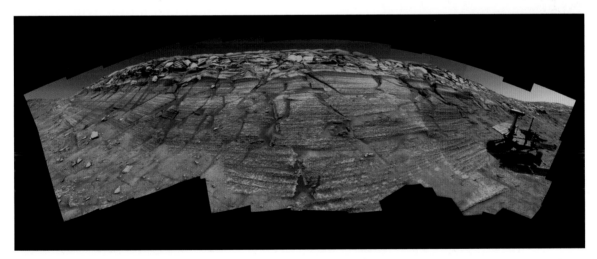

Opportunity rover on Mars

In 2003, two vehicles or '**rovers**', called *Spirit* and *Opportunity* landed on Mars. They have been driving around and taking pictures and samples of rock and soil to help scientists to find out much more about this planet. One of the things they have been trying to find is evidence that there might once have been life on Mars. We now believe there was once liquid water on the surface because we can see features that look like dry rivers. There might have been living things on the planet, but they would probably have been tiny things like bacteria. There certainly have never been little green men!

If people ever travel farther away from the Earth, Mars is the most likely place for them to go. It would take more than 5 months to get there and life would be quite difficult. The lack of water would be a problem and there is also no oxygen in the Martian atmosphere. As it is further from the Sun than Earth, it can be very cold maybe as low as -140 °C at the poles. Even the hottest day is below 20 °C, which is a comfortable room temperature on Earth.

Next on our journey would be **Jupiter**. The Romans named Jupiter after the king of their gods. Jupiter is the biggest of the planets. It is a huge ball of gas with a tiny rocky centre. There are huge storms on Jupiter. One of them is a massive swirling thunderstorm, about 25 000 km across, that may have been raging for over 300 years! This can be seen from Earth and is called the Great Red Spot. Jupiter has 63 moons that we know about.

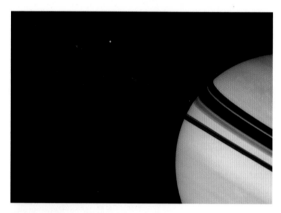

Saturn's moons, Cassini image

Saturn is the most easily recognisable planet because of its beautiful icy rings. Saturn is also a gas planet and is named after Jupiter's father who was the god of agriculture. In 1997, a space probe called Cassini was launched from Earth to go to Saturn. It arrived in 2004, a journey of 7 years! Cassini has sent back some beautiful pictures of Saturn and its moons.

Did you know?
Saturn is so light that it would float on water – if you could find a lake big enough to put it in!

The last two planets are called **Uranus** and **Neptune**. Uranus was the Roman god of the heavens and Neptune was their god of the sea. Both of these planets are spheres of gas and look blue. We don't know much about these planets because they are so far away. All the planets **rotate**. Apart from Uranus they rotate in such a way that each part of the planet is sometimes in light and sometimes in the dark. Uranus is rather strange because it seems to have toppled over so that one half is always in the dark and the other half is always in the light. Neptune has really dreadful weather, with winds blowing up to 2500 km per hour!

Beyond Neptune comes **Pluto**. Pluto used to be included as one of the planets but, in 2006, astronomers decided that it was too small to be counted as a proper planet so it is now called a 'dwarf planet'. There are probably several other rocky objects orbiting in the area just beyond Pluto and some of these are probably as big or even bigger than Pluto. They are so far away that we have not yet been able to study them.

To do: Planets

1. Make a planets fact book. You could work as teams in your class to make a planet page each or maybe do this on your own. Find out some interesting facts about each of the planets. For example, how far from the Sun they are, how long are their days and years, from what they are made, how many moons they have, how hot and cold they become. You could find a picture of each planet to illustrate your pages.

2. Find out more about what it might be like to land on Venus. Imagine that you are travelling to Venus and write a diary about your experiences. You could write about how you feel as you travel and what it feels like to pass through the clouds and land on the planet.

Exercise 8.2

1. What is the Sun?

2. How far away from Earth is the Sun?

3. How long does it take light to travel from the Sun to Earth?

4. How many planets are there in the solar system?

5. Which planets are closer to the Sun than the Earth?

6. Which planet is named after the Roman god of war?

7. How do we know so much about the planet you named in question 6?

8. Why is Earth the best place in the solar system for life to exist?

9. Which feature of Saturn makes it easy to identify?

10. Why is Pluto no longer considered to be a planet?

· ·

Exercise 8.3: Extension question

Imagine that you are the first person to land on Mars. Write a 'space postcard' home telling your family what it is like to be there.

· ·

Earth and Moon

The planet we know most about is, of course, the Earth. The Earth is a ball of rock surrounded by a thin layer of gas called the **atmosphere**. The atmosphere is made up mostly from the gases nitrogen and oxygen. About two-thirds of the Earth's surface is covered with water.

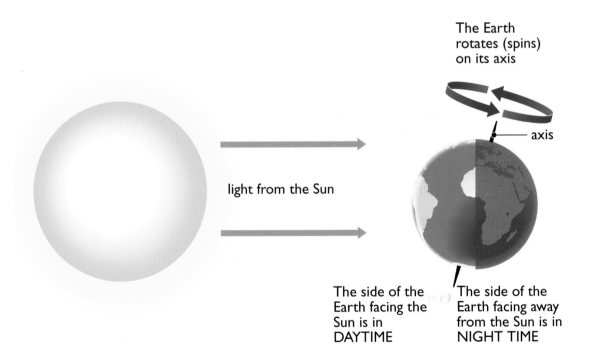

The Earth rotates (spins) on its axis

axis

light from the Sun

The side of the Earth facing the Sun is in DAYTIME

The side of the Earth facing away from the Sun is in NIGHT TIME

Day and night

As the Earth travels through space, it spins round and round on its **axis**. The axis is an imaginary stick passing right through the centre of the Earth. This means that each part of the Earth is sometimes facing towards the Sun and is sometimes facing away from the Sun. One complete **rotation** (spin) takes 24 hours. We call this amount of time a day. When we are facing towards the Sun, we are in daylight and when we face away from the Sun we are in darkness, night time.

The Earth spins round and round but the Sun stays in the same place. This means we have to look in different directions to see it. Because we cannot feel the Earth spinning, it seems to us that it is the Sun which is moving. The Sun seems to rise in the east in the morning and travel higher and higher across the sky until around mid-day, when it is to the south of us. It then seems to drop slowly to the west through the afternoon. (See Changing shadows, *Junior Science Book 1*, page 95.)

To do: Explaining day and night

Model how day and night happen

1. Use a big ball for the Earth and a lamp for the Sun. It is best if you can do this in a dark place.

2. Use the model to help you to explain what happens and then ask your partner to explain it to you.

3. Think about the two explanations. Can you make a really good explanation by putting together the best bits from yours and your partner's?

Explaining why the Sun moves across the sky

1. Use a lamp for the Sun.

2. Sit on a swivelling chair a little way from the lamp. Turn the chair so that the lamp is on your left.

3. Hold a card marked with compass points with east to your left and south pointing away from you and north pointing to your tummy. To see the lamp 'Sun' you now need to look towards the east. This is sunrise.

4. Without changing the position of the card, turn slowly in your chair anticlockwise (towards the lamp 'Sun'). Think about which direction you are looking in to see the 'Sun'. To help you with this, put a pointer on your card, and turn the pointer so that it is always pointing to the 'Sun' as you turn.

5. When you have turned a quarter of the way around, you should be facing the lamp 'Sun'. Which direction on your card are you facing now? This is mid-day.

7. Keep turning around until the 'Sun' is to your right (in the west). This is sunset. You have turned half way around.

8. Keep turning around. Soon you will find that you cannot see the lamp at all because it is behind you. This is night time.

9. As you keep turning you will return to where you started and the 'Sun' is again rising in the east. A new day has started.

The Earth takes about 365¼ days to travel in its orbit all the way round the Sun. This period of time is called a **year**. If you look at the diagram on page 137, you can see that the Earth is slightly tilted in relation to its orbit around the Sun, so that the North Pole is not exactly at the top and the South Pole is not exactly at the bottom. As the Earth moves around the Sun we find that the northern **hemisphere** (the 'top half of the Earth') is sometimes tilted towards the Sun and sometimes tilted away from the Sun. When it is tilted towards the Sun, the Sun seems higher in the sky and the light and heat are stronger. This is summer in Britain. Winter happens when the northern hemisphere is tilted away from the Sun. The Sun seems lower in the sky and the light and heat are not so strong so the weather gets colder.

Not all places have summer and winter. Places near the equator have temperatures and light that don't vary as much as they do in the UK. Can you think why?

Did you know?
The distance travelled by the Earth around the Sun is about 940 million kilometres. To travel this distance in a year we must be rushing through space at a speed of about 100 000 kilometres per hour!

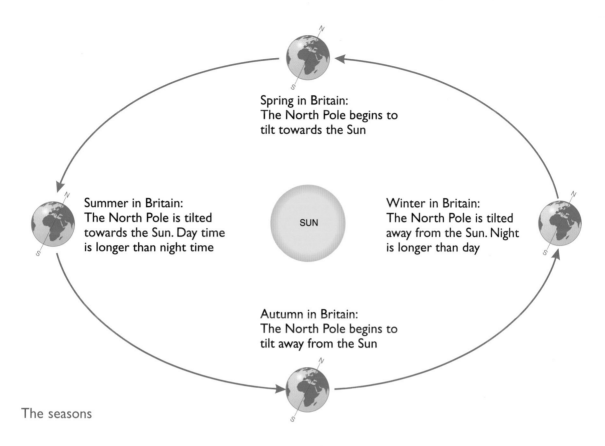

The seasons

The Moon is a sphere of rock that orbits the Earth. Many scientists believe the Moon was probably formed when a lump of rock about the size of Mars crashed into the Earth about 4½ billion years ago. It takes 28 days (a lunar month) for the Moon to orbit the Earth.

The Moon is a non-luminous object (does not make its own light) so we can only see it because light from the Sun is reflected off its surface.

The Moon spins like the Earth so there are days and nights on the Moon too. One day lasts exactly the same time as it takes the Moon to orbit the Earth so the same bit of the Moon is always facing us. We never see the other side from Earth. The only way we can find out what the other side of the Moon looks like is to send spacecraft to take pictures.

The Moon

To do: Make an orrery

An orrery is a model that shows the positions and movements of the planets and moons in the solar system. Here are the instructions to make a simple one showing the Sun, the Earth and the Moon.

1. Cut a square of card that will form the base of your orrery. You could cut this from black card and draw some stars on it.

2. Cut a circle of paper, a little smaller than your square. Mark the centre and draw lines through this to divide the circle into four equal quarters. Then divide each quarter into three, by drawing through the centre of the circle, to make twelve equal sections. Write the names of the months in each section in order, anticlockwise around the outer edge. Stick the circle onto the centre of the black card.

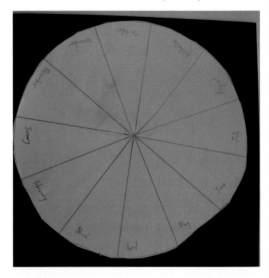

3. Cut a circle of card a little smaller than your paper circle. Mark the centre of the circle carefully and draw the Sun in the centre or make a Sun from coloured paper and stick it in the centre. Make a hole a little way in from the edge of this circle.

4. Draw a smaller circle on some card, mark the centre and then draw a little circle overlapping the edge of this circle. This little circle is the Moon, so colour it in to make it look like the Moon. Cut round the outside of this shape.

5. Lastly, cut out a small circle to represent the Earth. This must fit into the centre of your Moon circle. Colour it to look like the Earth and mark the centre.

6. To make your orrery, push a paper fastener through the centre of the Earth circle and then through the centre of the Moon circle. Push the fastener through the hole in the edge of the Sun circle and then open it up to fix these three pieces together.

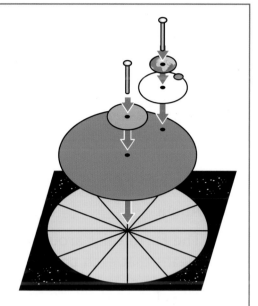

7. Take another paper fastener and push it through the mark in the centre of the Sun circle and then through the centre of the base card. Open it up to fix the orrery together.

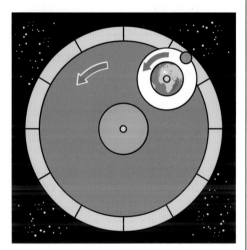

Your Earth can now orbit the Sun and you can make the Moon orbit the Earth. You could draw arrows on the circles to remind yourself that they both orbit in an anti-clockwise direction.

Exercise 8.4

Use the words in the box to fill in the gaps in the sentences below. Each word may be used once, more than once or not at all.

> luminous   axis   28 days   365¼   orbit   atmosphere
> light   space   non-luminous   day   darkness   reflected
> two-thirds   24 hours   year   sphere

1. The Earth is surrounded by a layer of gas called the _____ .

2. About _____ of the Earth's surface is covered in water.

3. The Earth spins around an imaginary stick called the _____ which means that each part of the Earth is sometimes in _____ and sometimes in _____ .

4. It takes _____ for the Earth to spin round once on its _____ . We call this a _____ .

5. The Earth takes about _____ days to orbit the Sun. We call this a _____ .

6. The Moon is a _____ of rock that orbits the Earth.

7. It takes _____ for the Moon to travel once round the Earth.

8. The Moon is _____ so we can only see it when light from the Sun is _____ off its surface.

. . . .

Exercise 8.5

1. Which two gases make up most of the Earth's atmosphere?

2. Draw a clearly labelled diagram to show how day and night are caused.

3. How many days does it take the Earth to orbit the Sun? What name is given to this period of time?

4. Explain in your own words why we have changing seasons in some places on Earth.

5. How do many scientists think that the Moon was made?

6. Explain how we can see the Moon even though it is non-luminous.

Index